SNIPS & SNAILS & WALNUT WHALES

Nature Crafts for Children

SNIPS&SNAILS&

Nature Crafts

WALNUT WHALES
for Children

by PHYLLIS FIAROTTA with NOEL FIAROTTA

WP WORKMAN PUBLISHING COMPANY
New York

Copyright © 1975 by Phyllis Fiarotta

Library of Congress Cataloging in Publication Data

Fiarotta, Phyllis.
    Snips & snails & walnut whales.

    SUMMARY: Instructions for making a variety of useful and decorative objects using raw materials from nature.
        1. Nature craft--Juvenile literature.
[1. Nature craft. 2. Handicraft] I. Fiarotta, Noel, joint author. II. Title.
TT160.F49   745.5   75-9574
ISBN 0-911104-75-5
ISBN 0-911104-49-6 pbk.

Workman Publishing Company .
231 East 51st Street
New York, New York 10022

Contributing editor: Noel Fiarotta
Illustrations: Phyllis Fiarotta
Book Designer: Bernard Springsteel
Cover: Paul Hanson
Photographs:
Color Photographs: Jerry Darvin
Black and white photographs: Ray Solwinski
Typeset: Vermont Photo-Tape
Printed and bound by the George Banta Co.
Manufactured in the United States of America

First printing, April 1975

To all children who are
part of my life,
especially those who
helped me with this book.
To Adam, Alan, Bridget,
Gina, Greg, Johnathon, Karren,
Kendra, Keven, Kyle,
Marc, Nicoletta and Scot.
And with a special
thought to all
the children of the
A. Harry Moore School.

Table of Contents

FOREWORD TO PARENTS 14

JUST FOR YOU 15

NATURE'S GIFTS AND WHERE TO FIND THEM 16

OTHER THINGS YOU'LL NEED 18

1. THE FLOWERS THAT BLOOM IN THE SPRING, TRA LA 21
    Daisy Chains 24
    Sachet Bags 26
    Flower Paperweights 28
    Still Life Paintings 30
    Floral Note Paper 32
    Flower Découpage 34
    Pussy Willow Paintings 36
    Stained Glass Collages 38

2. GREEN IS A LEAF'S SPECIAL COLOR 39
    Leaf Printing 42
    Leaf Stenciling 44
    Leaf Rubbings 46
    Leaf Casting 48
    Fern in a Candle 50
    Wax Leaf Ropes 52
    Placemats and Coasters 54
    Glycerin Leaves 56
    Lucky Clover Bookmarks 58

3. **TWIGS ARE PRESENTS FROM A TREE** .... .59
    Charm Mobile .... .62
    Gumdrop Tree .... .64
    Tomahawk .... .66
    Eye of God .... .68
    Picture Frame .... .70
    Tepee .... .72
    Log Cabin .... .74
    Bird Feeder .... .76
    Fishing Pole and Bow and Arrow .... .78

4. **A PINE CONE IS A NURSERY FOR SEEDS** .... .79
    Wild Bird Feeder .... .82
    Feathered Friends .... .84
    Pine Cone Elves .... .86
    Cone Flowers .... .88
    Candle Holder .... .90
    Door Wreath .... .92
    Tall Tree .... .94
    Small Christmas Tree .... .96

5. **BEANS, NUTS, AND SEEDS BEFORE THEY GROW UP** .... .97
    Walnut Ships .... .100
    Walnut Animals .... .102
    Walnut Photo Case .... .104
    Acorn Grapes .... .106
    Nut Tree .... .108
    Bean Layering .... .110
    Hobnail Glasses .... .112
    Bean Bags .... .114
    Birdseed Squiggles .... .116
    Seeded Pencil Holder Can .... .118
    Melon Seed Necklace .... .120

6. **WHICH CAME FIRST, THE CHICKEN OR THE EGG?** .... .121
    Blown Eggs .... .124
    Batik Eggs .... .126

Patchwork Eggs 128
Egg Paperweights 130
Egg Characters 132
Egg Village 134
Pot of Tulips 136
Egg Shell Mosaic 138
Egg Tree 140

7. STONES CAN BE FOUND EVERYWHERE 141
Rock Collection 144
Indian Pebble Game 146
Basket of Fruit 148
People and Pets 150
Stone Sculptures 152
Rock Pendant 154
Mosaic in Plaster 156
Stone Paperweights 158

8. A SHELL WAS ONCE A HOME 159
Shell Necklace and Pin 162
Slowpoke Turtle 164
Butterfly Mobile 166
Shell Flowers 168
Picture Frame 170
Standing Planter 172
Collage Box 174
Shell Comb 176

9. SAND IS A BLANKET BY THE SEA 177
Super Sand Castle 180
Sand-Casted Sun 182
Fantasy Sculptures 184
Apple Pin Cushion 186
Bubble Bird Cage 188
Sand Pouring 190
Sand Painting 192
Sand Dried Flowers 194

        Cactus Terrarium 196

10. FRUIT IS A BEAUTIFUL SWEET 197
        Caramel Apple Friends 200
        Apple—Head Puppets 202
        Fruit Printing 204
        Orange Pomander Ball 206
        Pear People 208
        Canned Fruit Animals 210
        Berry Ink 212
        Cranberry Necklace 214

11. EVEN YOU CAN LOVE VEGETABLES 215
        Carrot Necklace 218
        Colored Celery Tree 220
        Painted Pumpkins and Gourds 222
        Popcorn Painting 224
        Artichoke Flowers 226
        Potato Face 228
        Potato Printing 230
        Sweet Potato Plant 232

12. NATURE IS FILLED WITH WONDROUS THINGS 233
        Feathered Peace Pipe 236
        Salt Play Clay 238
        Wheat Sunburst 240
        Corn Husk Doll 242
        Sponge Printing 244
        Sugar Rock Candy 246
        Crystal Garden 248
        Mushroom Prints 250
        Web Painting 252
        Rain-Spatter Painting 254
        Two Happy Snowmen 256
        Wishbone Pendant 258

13. *THE SMOOTH, SHINY, SLIPPERY STONE* 259
    Oak Tree and Smooth, Shiny, Slippery Stone 262
    Owl and Molly Mole 264
    Squirrel and Mr. Turtle 266
    A Special Play for You to Perform—*The Smooth, Shiny, Slippery Stone* 269
    GOODBYE—"I CREATE WITH NATURE" MEDAL 282

Foreword to parents

This is a book of nature crafts for children. It shows how nature provides the artist or craftsman with raw materials as well as the sense of form, color, and harmony from which all beautiful or useful things are born. In making the projects found here, your children explore the relationship between natural things and the created object and come to know nature better while learning to use it in new and imaginative ways.

SNIPS & SNAILS & WALNUT WHALES belongs to the youth of today. It is written for children to understand. All specific measurements (inches and feet) are omitted, leaving the total creative process to the young artisan. Drawings accompany each craft project, and in some cases step-by-step illustrations are included. No guesswork is needed.

Some crafts will appeal to your children, others less so. Don't force them, just for creativity's sake, to make something they won't use. Let them decide which projects interest them most. They will automatically select the things most appropriate to their age group. Your children know themselves very well and what it is they most enjoy making.

The adult plays an important part in the construction process. Read through this book before you hand it over to your children. Look at all the craft items and see how the instructions are written. **You will notice the symbol ** in front of a direction. This means that potentially dangerous household equipment is called for, or that the execution of the step so marked may be too difficult for a child.** It is advisable for you to supervise this activity. Keep in mind your children's physical abilities and limitations. If you feel they cannot perform a particular task, you will have to do it for them. Allow youngsters to feel, however, that they are the ones creating the objects, even though it is you who have just bored a hole in a piece of cardboard or cut a length of string.

Every craft item in this book is presented in three parts: the drawing, the instructions, and a list of craft materials. Children should be encouraged to read through the instructions several times before they begin, and to study the drawings carefully. You will provide them with the necessary craft supplies and help them gather natural materials. Craft supplies can be bought in a stationery or art supply store, or at the stationery counter of department stores. Other items will be found in your kitchen or in the family tool box. Shop around in the woods, by the seashore, or in your backyard for twigs, rocks, sand, and any of the other natural craft supplies required. Every trip away from home can be a productive nature supply gathering involving the entire family. Don't forget to save all leftover items for future craft projects.

You and your children live in a time of renewed awareness of natural things and of the need for their conservation. We have learned the importance of the word "recycle" as it concerns the wise use of "waste" materials.

The craft boom has done its part to show us how our material resources may be reused constructively. This book should help take you and your children further in this direction, encouraging work which will create a real sense of accomplishment in its completion and display. With a little patience and devotion, all of the crafts in this book will become the natural wonders of your children's world.

Just for you

Starting at this moment, try to be aware of every natural object in front, above, and under you. Let the breeze part your hair and go grab a handful of autumn leaves. Gather stones, sand, shells, pine cones—any of nature's fascinating creations. Now you can use these earthly wonders to create beautiful things for you, your family, and friends. This book will open the gates to Mother Nature's wonderful kingdom.

There are many interesting crafts to make using natural craft materials like sand, snow, and flowers. Create a bouquet of dried flowers for the dining room table, a sand-casted plaster sunburst for your room, or a pine cone bird feeder for your feathered friends.

Look through the book and decide which craft item you would like to make first. It is very important that you read all directions not just once, but several times before you begin. If there is something you don't understand, have someone explain it to you. It is important that you study the drawings as well. You will be better able to understand the directions if you see how a craft is put together.

Your mom and dad will be very helpful to you. They will buy and help you find all the materials you will need for the projects you choose. If you have difficulty cutting, threading, sewing, or doing anything, ask for a helping hand. Once you learn the proper way to handle tools and materials, the construction of the items will be easier.

By now you should be as eager as a beaver to get started. Find a project you want to construct, and head for the hills in search of the natural things you'll need. Nature will provide enough craft materials for everyone (though you should never take more at one time than you actually require). Once you get going on the craftwork, you'll probably find it difficult to stop. That's the great thing about this book—reading it is like floating down a winding river with new treasures appearing at every turn of the shore.

Nature's gifts and where to find them

Nature's gifts can be found in the backyard, saved from trips to the beach or gathered on hikes and family picnics. It is a good idea to collect the gifts as you find them and to store them in a special place until you need them for a craft project. Try to keep your craft shelf well-stocked. If you need to supplement your craft supplies, many of the natural materials can be purchased from florists or in craft and hobby stores.

FLOWERS

• **Flowers** grow in fields or gardens, almost everywhere in nature. People who live in warm climates will have field flowers for a longer period of time than those living in cooler places. A florist can supply you with flowers anytime of the year, of course.

LEAVES

• **Leaves** grow on tree branches, bushes, vegetables, and flower stems. Tree leaves are best for the craft projects in this book. Fern and many evergreen branches, also needed for some of the projects, may be purchased from your local florist during any season.

TWIGS

• **Twigs** are small shoots or branches from trees or certain shrubs. Try not to remove twigs from living trees, but wait until they can be gathered from fallen branches. Certain "twigs" can be found along the seashore. These twigs are actually smooth wooden branches called driftwood—wood that is drifted or floated by the sea.

PINE CONES

• **Pine cones** are the seed carriers of pine trees. Other trees grow cones—like the larch and the spruce. The next time you pass a pine, spruce, or larch, look under the tree for fallen cones.

SEEDS, BEANS, AND NUTS

• **Seeds, beans, and nuts** are usually found in your kitchen—it's the first place to look. Fruits like oranges and melons contain seeds; some cooking spices are seeds, like unground mustard. Wild birdseed or parakeet seed can be bought at the five-and-ten-cent store, or at your local grocery. Dried beans and shelled nuts are also available at the food store. If you are more adventurous and live in the country, gather nuts in the woods. You can find acorns, black walnuts, and hickory nuts during the fall.

EGGS

• **Eggs** come from many kinds of birds, but we will use only chicken eggs for craft projects. These are sold in grocery stores, as you must know, by the carton.

STONES

• **Stones** can be found in all shapes, sizes, and colors almost everywhere you look in the outdoor world. Smooth white stones, sometimes called for in the projects, can be found at the seashore.

SHELLS

• **Shells** are best found by the seashore. Clams, oysters, and other shellfish can be bought at the fish market or in large supermarkets; enjoy eating them and then save the shells. Restaurants that specialize in fish dinners will also have a good supply of shells which should be available for the asking. Florists and hobby stores sell packages of pretty shells and there are the newer shell shops which carry all kinds of shells exclusively.

SAND

• **Sand** is found at the seashore or the desert. It can be bought at the hardware store or the florist.

FRUIT AND VEGETABLES

• **Fruits and vegetables** are usually found at the supermarket or grocery store. Some varieties are available only at special times of the year, while you can get others all year long. There may be a tree in your garden that produces fruit, or a plant that bears vegetables.

Other things you'll need

PAPER

• **White drawing paper** is important in craft projects as well as for drawing. Drawing paper is heavy, smooth paper that comes in pads or packages.

• **Colored construction paper** is heavy paper that comes in many wonderful colors. The sheets are sold in packages, and many paper sizes are available. Try to pick the correct size for the craft you will be making. Save all large scraps in a box or bag. You never know when you might need a little bit of color.

• **Tracing paper** is a light, transparent paper. When it is placed on a drawing, you can see the drawing through it. Tracing paper comes in pads.

• **Typewriter paper** is a white paper that is lighter than white drawing paper but heavier than tracing paper. You can see a drawing under it. It comes in packaged sheets.

• **Cardboard** is very heavy paper. You can find it backing shirts which come from the laundry or in packages of new clothes. Other boxes found around the house—like shoe and hat boxes—are made of it. Cardboard may also be bought in art supply stores. **Oaktag** is a kind of cardboard which you will probably have to buy; it comes in large sheets and is available at stationery and art supply stores. Save all pieces of cardboard you find in your home.

GLUES AND PASTES

• **Liquid white glue** comes in plastic bottles with pointed caps. This glue makes a strong bond when it dries and is used, therefore, for hard-to-glue crafts.

• **Paper paste** is a white, thick adhesive. It comes usually in a jar, and has a plastic spreader. Paper paste is best for sticking paper to paper.

COLORINGS

• **Poster paints** are paints that can be removed from your hands with water. They come in many colors and are sold in jars.

• **Watercolor paints** are little tablets of hard color that must be daubed with a wet brush to use. The paints come in a tin which has at least six colors in it.

• **Crayons** are colored wax sticks that are used for drawing.

• **Colored felt-tipped markers** are tubes or "pencils" of enclosed watercolor with a felt coloring tip. You draw with markers as you would with crayons.

FABRIC

• **Felt** is a strong, heavy fabric that comes in many colors. It is sold in small squares. It can be glued to a surface with liquid white glue.

• **Scrap fabric** is odds and ends of cloth that your mom saves from her sewing projects. You can also cut up old clothes for scrap fabric.

MOULDING MATERIALS

• **Plaster of paris** is a white powdery substance which, when united with water, hardens as it drys. It is available at hardware stores.

• **Paraffin** is a waxy material sold usually in blocks at supermarkets, hardware, and five-and-ten-cent stores. It is melted, and used for home canning or candle making.

• **Play clay** is any non-hardening modeling clay which comes in colors and is available at hobby, art supply, and five-and-ten-cent stores.

The flowers that bloom in the spring, tra la

The flowers that bloom in the spring, tra la

Spring is perhaps the most magical of all the seasons. Nature performs one of her really miraculous tricks. Right before your very eyes, flowers and leaves seem to pop out everywhere. Just as the magician pulls a rabbit out of his hat, so spring changes the gray of winter into a starburst of color. You see and smell new life almost everywhere you go—feel new yourself.

Spring is just one part of nature's year-long mystery. After spring there's summer, during which all growing things flourish. Come autumn, flowers and leaves begin to die, but with their own subtle or brilliant colors going that make the world maybe even more beautiful than before. In the winter nature rests and the earth regains its strength. Then it's time for spring again, and those wonderful flowers that bloom, tra la.

If you like spring—to see, touch, and smell flowers—then this chapter is for you. With it, you'll capture spring's colors and be able to display their beauty all year long. Many of the projects here require flowers that have been dried—the book will tell you how—so you might want to start a dried flower collection now. Begin by gathering either garden or wild flowers (better ask Mom or Dad first if you intend to raid the garden), dry and save them for future craft use. After you have made some or all of the projects in this chapter you should know flowers better than ever. It's an acquaintanceship that's really nice to have.

Daisy Chains

As far back as two thousand years ago, people decorated their heads with flowers and leaves. You won't see many people walking around your neighborhood with flowers in their hair these days. In some countries, however, people still use flowers to decorate the top parts of their bodies.

The daisy chain is a craft you should do in the early summer; the daisy is in bloom at this time. If you live in an area where daisies don't grow, any flower with a long stem will do. The daisy is a wild flower, and can frequently be seen growing along the sides of country roads. Pick only enough daisies to use for this project. You wouldn't want to leave the countryside bare of flowers.

Things You Need

scissors
freshly picked daisies
butter knife
paper clip

Let's Begin

1. Cut daisies leaving a stem that is about as long as your hand.
**2. Starting a little way from the bottom, cut a small slit through all the stems, Fig. a. Make sure not to cut all the way through the bottom of the stem.
3. Pass the stem of one daisy through the slit of another, Fig. b. Pull the second stem all the way through the first.
4. Take a third daisy and pass it through the slit of the second daisy, Fig. c.
5. Continue by passing a new stem through the slit of the last attached daisy until you have a chain of daisies.
6. When you have made a chain as long as you want, attach the last stem to the stem of the first daisy with a paper clip. Try making a chain from other kinds of flowers, or mixing kinds in a single chain.

Sachet Bags

If you smell a pretty fragrance in a closet or drawer, it might mean that there is a sachet bag somewhere present. You can buy sachet bags—little cloth pouches filled with fragrant herbs and flowers—in stores, but it is much more fun to make one. Your room, bureau drawers, or closet will smell sweeter after you have finished this project.

Things You Need

flowers
scissors
shoe box or gift box with a lid
see-through fabric or netting
needle and thread
dime-store cologne
ribbon

Let's Begin

1. Collect roses or other flowers that smell sweet.
2. Cut away the stems and leaves with scissors.
3. Place the flowers in a shoe box or a gift box and cover.
4. Place the box in a dark, dry place like a closet or an attic.
5. Allow the flowers to dry for ten days.
6. Cut two rectangular shapes out of the fabric which are exactly the same size—the length of each shape should be longer than its width.
**7. Thread a needle with sewing thread, and knot the ends of the thread together.
8. Place the two fabric shapes together.
**9. Using a running stitch, sew down one of the long sides a little in from the edge. To make a running stitch, first push the needle through both pieces of fabric near the top of one side and pull the thread until it is stopped by the knot. Now push the needle back through both pieces of fabric a little way from the knot. Continue to pass the needle back and forth through the fabric making small, equally spaced stitches, Fig. a.
10. Now sew along the bottom leaving some extra fabric between your sewing and the bottom edge, Fig. b. Complete the bag by sewing up the other side. The last stitch should be sewn several times. Cut away the extra thread.
11. Cut slits into the extra fabric on the bottom of the bag to make a fringe, Fig. c. Be sure not to cut into the sewn stitches.
12. Sprinkle a little of the cologne on the completely dried flowers.
13. Fill the bag half-full of the dried flowers.
14. Tie the top of the bag with a ribbon and make a bow.

Flower Paperweights

A paperweight can be used by every member of your family. Dad can use one for his desk. Mom can use one in the kitchen to keep her bills in one place. Your sister or brother can use one for keeping homework papers together. You will have to read Sand-Dried Flowers, page 194, to make the dried flowers you will need for this project. You will need quite a few if you are going into the paperweight business—something you may find yourself doing after people get a look at one of these floral beauties.

Things You Need

glass ashtray or small jar with a lid
colored construction paper
pencil
scissors
liquid white glue
sand-dried flowers, see page 194
waxed paper

Let's Begin

1. Turn the ashtray upside down and place it on a sheet of colored construction paper.
2. Trace around the edge with a pencil, Fig. a.
3. Cut out the tracing with scissors, Fig. b.
4. Glue one or several of the sand-dried flowers on the cutout tracing.
5. Let the glue dry completely on the paper.
6. Place the paper with the flower on top of a piece of waxed paper, which will protect your working surface.
7. Squeeze liquid white glue along the edges of the construction paper cutout, Fig. c.
8. Fit the upside down ashtray onto the wet glue, matching the shape of the ashtray to that of the paper as exactly as you can.
9. Allow the paperweight to dry completely before you handle it.
10. Or, if you are using a jar with a lid, proceed as follows: Glue the flower to the inside of the jar lid. When the flower has dried in place, carefully screw the jar onto the lid, see illustration.

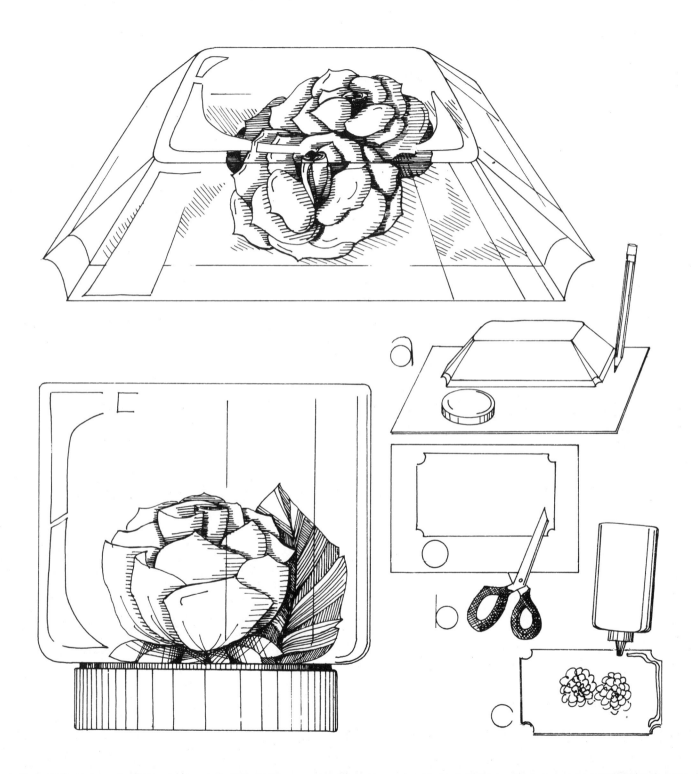

Still Life Paintings

Still life paintings show things that are inanimate—things which don't move—such as a bowl of fruit. You won't be painting in this project, but you *will* create a painting using dried flowers. Dried flowers retain some of their original color and make a beautiful picture when placed on a piece of colored construction paper.

Things You Need

scissors
cardboard, preferably oaktag
colored construction paper
paper paste
liquid white glue
sand-dried flowers, see page 194
colored felt-tipped marker or crayon

Let's Begin

1. Cut a piece of cardboard any size you wish.

2. Cut a piece of colored construction paper smaller than the cardboard. The paper should be cut so that when it is placed in the center of the cardboard, an equal amount of cardboard border shows on all four sides.
3. Center the paper on the cardboard and paste down.
4. Cut out a vase shape from colored construction paper.
5. Paste the vase near the bottom of the colored paper background, see illustration.
6. Glue a bouquet of dried flowers over the vase shape using large dots of the liquid white glue to fasten the flowers. Be careful that the flowers do not crumble as you work.
7. Cut a paper sign to fit on the cardboard border. Using the felt-tipped marker or a crayon, write your name and where you picked the flowers on the sign.
8. Paste the sign onto the cardboard border.
9. Glue a paper or a ribbon bow on the vase.

Flowers picked
and dried by
ANDREW KENE

Floral Note Paper

One of the nicest presents you can receive is a box of pretty stationery. Writing letters on special paper is somehow more enjoyable, makes you feel like you're sending more of yourself with every message. If you don't have a box of personal stationery why not design your own? Gather flowers, preferably of the daisy type rather than the rose. Flat flowers can be pressed more easily than bulky flowers. You might want to make extra sheets for gifts or even for display.

Things You Need

freshly picked flowers, leaves or ferns
white drawing paper
heavy books
envelopes
scissors
liquid white glue
paper cup
paintbrush
tweezers
colored construction paper
waxed paper

Let's Begin

1. Place "flat" flowers like daisies, leaves or ferns between two sheets of drawing paper.
2. Place the paper with the flowers between the pages of a heavy book, Fig. a.
3. Place more books on top of the first, Fig. b.
4. Let the flowers dry in the book for ten days.
5. After ten days, remove the paper and flowers.
6. To make a piece of note paper, fold white drawing paper in half. Trim the paper to fit the size of the envelope you will use. Do not cut away the folded edge.
7. Pour a little liquid white glue into a paper cup.
8. Using the paintbrush, paint the back of the pressed flowers with the glue.
9. Remove the flowers from the paper with tweezers, and glue them onto the top fold side of the paper, Fig. c. For fancier note paper, glue a strip of colored construction paper down the folded side. Glue the flowers onto this border.
10. Place a sheet of waxed paper over the note paper and put both in a book to dry overnight.
11. Write a note to a friend when the flower note paper has completely dried.

Dear Fred,
    I want you to know that I made this card
my
fo
Ih

Dear Fred,
    I want you
to Know that
I made this card

Grandma,
Last week
mom took
us to pick
buttercups.
We picked
them and
put them
in a heavy
book. Mom →

a

b

c

Flower Découpage

Découpage is a way of decorating an object with pictures, cutouts or, in this case, flowers. The decoration is protected and made to look beautiful by coatings of a clear, hard finish. With a plate, dried flowers, and liquid white glue, you will make a beautiful découpaged craft that will look great in any room of your house. After you see how pretty your first project looks, you will be découpaging everything in sight.

Things You Need

book-dried flowers, leaves or ferns, see page 32
white paper or plastic plate
crayons
liquid white glue
paper cup
paintbrush
tweezers
plastic wrap or aluminum foil
stick-on picture hanger

Let's Begin

1. Start by making book-dried flowers, see page 32.
2. Decorate the inside rim of the plate with a crayon design.
3. Pour liquid white glue into a paper cup.
4. Paint the bottom of the inside of the plate with a coating of the glue, Fig. a.
5. Using the tweezers, carefully pick up the dried flowers and leaves from the paper. Arrange them on the glued surface.
6. Paint over the flowers with a light coating of glue, Fig. b.
7. Allow the glue to dry completely. While the plate is drying, cover the glue in the cup with plastic wrap or foil.
8. Give the entire plate a second coating of glue after the first coating has dried.
9. When dry, stick a picture hanger on the back of the plate to hang.

Pussy Willow Paintings

You know it's spring when you see pussy willows around. You probably think that they are meant for putting in vases only, but a beautiful form of painting can be done with the buds of pussy willow branches. In some areas of this country you can go out into the woods in the spring and find pussy willow. In most cases, however, you will have to buy branches of pussy willow from the florist.

Things You Need

white drawing paper
pencil
colored felt-tipped markers or crayons
pussy willow buds
liquid white glue
paper cup
paintbrush

Let's Begin

1. Draw a very simple design on a piece of drawing paper with a pencil, see the illustration for an example.
2. Color the drawing with felt-tipped markers or crayons. You can also make a drawing with pieces of colored construction paper cut into various shapes and pasted to the drawing paper.
3. Remove pussy willow buds from their branches.
4. Pour liquid white glue into a paper cup.
5. Paint an area on your picture with white glue.
6. Place pussy willow buds on the glued area.
7. Continue gluing pussy willow buds, wherever you want them on your picture.
8. Allow the pussy willow buds to dry.
9. The pussy willow buds can be tinted using colored felt-tipped markers.

Stained Glass Collages

One of the most beautiful of all the art forms is stained glass. Churches all over the world are famous for their stained glass windows, and many old homes have small stained glass windows above their doors or elsewhere around the house. If you like stained glass windows, here is a craft that will give you something of the experience of making them yourself.

You won't be working with real glass, however. Flowers will form the basis of your picture. Waxed paper will seal the flowers down to produce the stained glass effect. You can hang several of these collages on your window or frame them for your bedroom wall.

Things You Need

white drawing paper

newspaper
waxed paper
book-dried flowers, see page 32
crayons
pencil or crayon sharpener
glitter (available at hobby or art supply stores)
iron

Let's Begin

1. Place a sheet of drawing paper on top of a piece of newspaper.
2. Place a sheet of waxed paper on top of the drawing paper. Arrange book-dried flowers, see page 32, on the waxed paper.
3. Remove the protective paper covering from old crayons and sharpen them over the flowers. Let the shavings fall evenly over the flowers.
4. Scatter glitter over the flowers and shavings.
5. Place a second sheet of waxed paper over the flowers and the decorations.
**6. Seal the two sheets together with an iron set at a low temperature.
7. "Hang" the collage in a bright window with tape.

Green
is a leaf's
special color

Green is a leaf's special color

It's difficult to imagine the earth without nature's green—all the living green things which make it beautiful (and actually produce, through a process called photosynthesis, the oxygen we need to live). A tree growing out of the city pavement is a lovely green sight. The hills of the country are beautiful for, among other things, the many shades of green that extend from the valley to the top of the highest peaks. Nature has given the earth a soothing color to look at every day of the year, even in the cold of winter, when pine trees add their green color to snowy days.

Although green is for looking at, it is also for making wonderful crafts. The green we are concerned with here is that of the leaf, which provides us with many interesting project ideas. If you study a leaf very closely you will see a highway of veins. For the person who likes to paint or draw in lines, a leaf rubbing of this network is just what the doctor ordered. Leaves can be used to decorate things, and this chapter will show you how to stencil and print with them. You'll even be able to make a leaf "fossil" or leaf impression cast in plaster.

When you are gathering leaves, look for unusual shapes, different sizes, and different colors. Don't pick more leaves than you need— trees look funny if too many leaves are missing from them. You might start looking out the window for leaves right now, and when you go out bring a paper bag for collecting leaves with you. Invite your friends to join you on your leaf safari.

41

Leaf Printing

When you hear the word "printing," what comes to mind? Most likely it is putting words on a piece of paper by means of type. There are many kinds of printing using many different things to make impressions: sponges, carved wood, and carved potatoes. This project uses leaves to make prints. You will be amazed to discover how many different leaf printings you can make.

Things You Need

liquid white glue
tree leaves
cardboard
poster paint or an ink pad
paintbrush
white drawing paper

Let's Begin

1. Squeeze liquid white glue around the edges of the top side of a leaf, Fig. a. The top side of the leaf is the smoother of the sides—the one without raised veins or stem.
2. Glue the leaf onto a piece of cardboard, Fig. b.
3. Allow the leaf to dry on the cardboard.
4. "Ink" the leaf by painting a thin coating of poster paint on it, Fig. c., or by pressing the leaf surface onto an ink pad.
5. Make a leaf printing by pressing the "inked" side of the leaf onto a sheet of drawing paper. Press heavily on the cardboard.
6. Carefully lift the cardboard, Fig. d. Repeat the process as many times as you want for various design effects. Make other printers with differently shaped leaves.

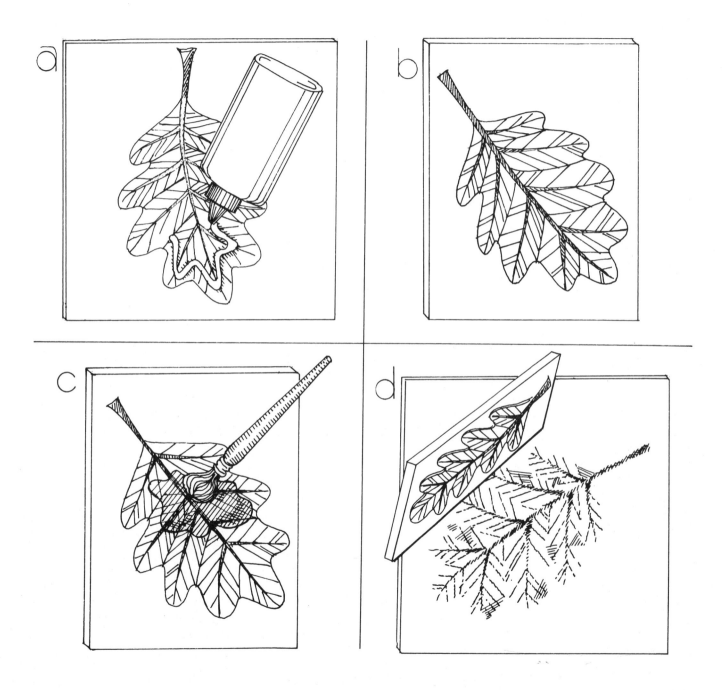

Leaf Stenciling

When was the last time you had to stencil something? It might have been a lettered heading for a homework assignment for school. The letters of the alphabet are stamped out of heavy cardboard in this kind of stencil and all you do is trace around the outline of the cutout letter with a pencil or pen. You can use leaves as stencils too. Gather all kinds of leaves, and you can make as many stencils as you want. You can stencil book covers, homework reports, or anything that needs nature's touch.

Things You Need

newspaper
paintbrush
poster paints
paper plate
sponge
tree leaves
white drawing paper
straight pins
old toothbrush
ice-cream stick

Let's Begin

SPONGE STENCILING
1. Spread newspaper over your working area to protect it.
2. Using a paintbrush, brush a little poster paint into the paper plate.
3. Wet a sponge, then squeeze all of the water out of it.
4. Place a leaf on a sheet of drawing paper.
5. Dip one end of the sponge into the paint. Dab the sponge up and down to get an even coating of paint on the sponge's surface.
6. Holding the leaf in place with your fingers, dab the painted side of the sponge over the leaf's edges and onto the paper, Fig. a.
7. Lift the leaf carefully to reveal the stenciled design.

SPATTER STENCILING
**1. Pin a leaf onto a piece of drawing paper with straight pins.
2. Pour a little poster paint into the plate.
3. Dip an old toothbrush into the paint. Shake off excess paint.
4. Holding the toothbrush over the leaf, rub the ice-cream stick across the bristles of the brush. The paint will spatter over the leaf and paper, Fig. b. Cover the paper around the leaf with spattering.
5. When the paint is dry, remove the pins and lift the leaf. Try spattering different colors of paint on top of one another for interesting effects.

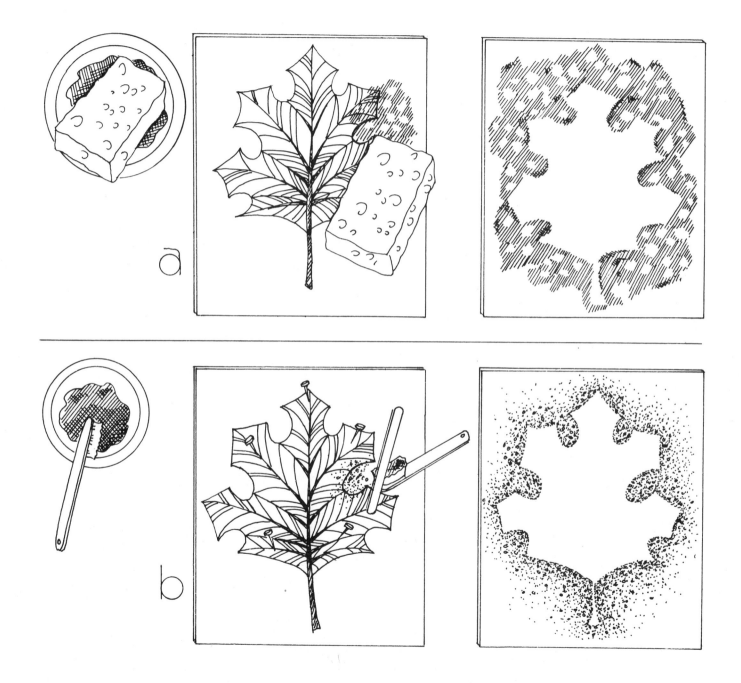

Leaf Rubbings

Making rubbings of different things can be a lot of fun. If you put a coin behind a piece of paper and rub a pencil over the paper where it covers the coin, an image of the coin will appear. What happens is that the raised surfaces of the coin "catch" the pencil strokes while lower surfaces do not. You may have done rubbings like this with other objects, but have you ever tried it with leaves? If you haven't, then you are in for some fun.

Things You Need

liquid white glue
tree leaves
typewriter paper or other lightweight paper
crayons

Let's Begin

1. Squeeze liquid white glue around the edges of the top side of several leaves, Fig. a. The top side of the leaf is the smoother of the sides—the one without raised veins or stem.
2. Glue the leaves onto a sheet of the paper, Fig. b. The raised sides of the leaves should face you.
3. Allow the leaves to dry.
4. Place another sheet of paper over the leaves, Fig. c.
5. Remove the protective paper covering from an old crayon.
6. Rub over the surface of the top paper with the side of the crayon, Fig. d. The veins and shape of the leaf under your rubbing will appear. Try using different colors of crayon for the different leaves, or for different parts of a single leaf.

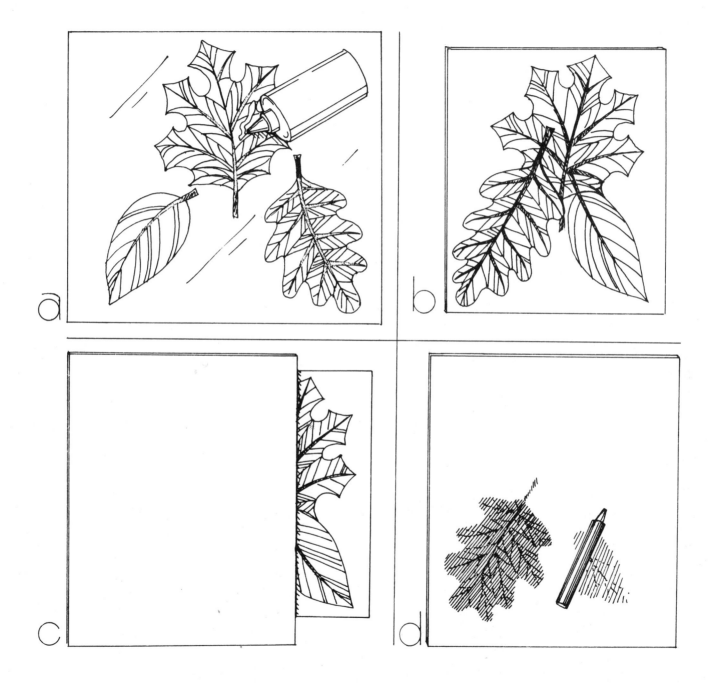

Leaf Casting

Millions of years ago, dinosaurs roamed the earth. When they were thirsty, they went to the rivers and streams for a drink of water. Little did they know they would leave something behind them that is still around today: their footprints in the mud. Over the years the mud hardened, and we can still see the size and shape of the dinosaurs' feet today. These hardened impressions are called fossils, and you can make something like them using leaves. All you need is plaster of paris, a little water, and a few minutes for drying. You won't have to wait millions of years for "fossils" of your own making.

Things You Need

disposable pie tin
large tin can
tree leaves
plaster of paris
spoon
paper clip
poster paint or watercolor paints (optional)

Let's Begin

1. Fill the pie tin with water, then pour the water into the can. Fill the pie tin again, this time half full, and add the water to the can.

2. Wet the top or smooth side of the leaf and stick it to the bottom of the disposable pie tin, Fig. a. The underneath or veined side of the leaf should face you.
3. Stirring all the while, add enough plaster of paris to the water in the can to make a mixture resembling loose whipped cream. Work as quickly as you can, and blend thoroughly.
4. Spoon some of the plaster of paris mixture onto the center of the leaf and spread it over the leaf until the leaf is covered, Fig. b.
5. Fill the pie tin with the remaining plaster of paris, Fig. c.
6. Set a paper clip into the plaster near the edge of the filled tin so that half of the clip remains in the plaster and half over the edge of the tin. The looped end of the clip will be used to hang the finished project.
7. In a half hour, remove the plaster carefully from the pie tin. The plaster is dry when it feels cool to the touch.
8. For an all-white casting, peel the leaf away now, Fig. d.
9. For a colored casting, paint the plaster before you peel away the leaf. When you remove the leaf, the leaf's impression will be white against a colored background.
10. Hang the casting by the paper-clip loop.

a

b

c

d

Fern in a Candle

Before Thomas Edison perfected the electric light bulb, and before the era of gaslight, people used candles as a source of light. People worked, ate, and read by flickering candles. Today, candles are found on top of birthday cakes, in churches, and as decorations in your home; you may even have one in your room. If you don't, here is a project that combines two of nature's products: wax and ferns.

Things You Need

scissors
pint or milk carton
butter
play clay (any non-hardening clay)
candle
2 saucepans, one larger than the other
small tin can
paraffin (canning wax)
fern

Let's Begin

1. Cut off the top part of a pint carton or half a milk carton, Fig. a.
2. Wash and dry the carton and butter the inside.
3. Place a ball of clay in the center of the bottom of the carton.
4. Choose a candle about as high as the cut carton.
5. Push the candle in the ball of clay at the bottom of the carton. The candle should stand up straight, Fig. b.
6. Fill the larger saucepan half full of water, and place on the stove.
7. Put the tin can in the center of the saucepan.
8. Add paraffin to the smaller saucepan.
9. Put the smaller saucepan into the larger. It should rest on the can in the water, Fig. c.
**10. Put the saucepan arrangement on a top burner of your stove. Turn on the stove carefully to a medium heat. The wax in the upper pot will melt slowly as the water begins to heat. Never take your eyes away from the melting wax.
11. When the wax has just melted, turn off the heat.
12. Put a fern into the carton. Trim the top if it comes above the edge of the carton.
**13. Carefully pour the melted wax into the carton, and up to the candlewick, Fig. d. Be sure the fern stands up straight.
**14. If you have not melted enough paraffin to fill the carton, allow the wax to harden in the carton before you melt and then add more wax.
15. When the wax has hardened completely, peel away the carton to unmold your candle, Fig. e.

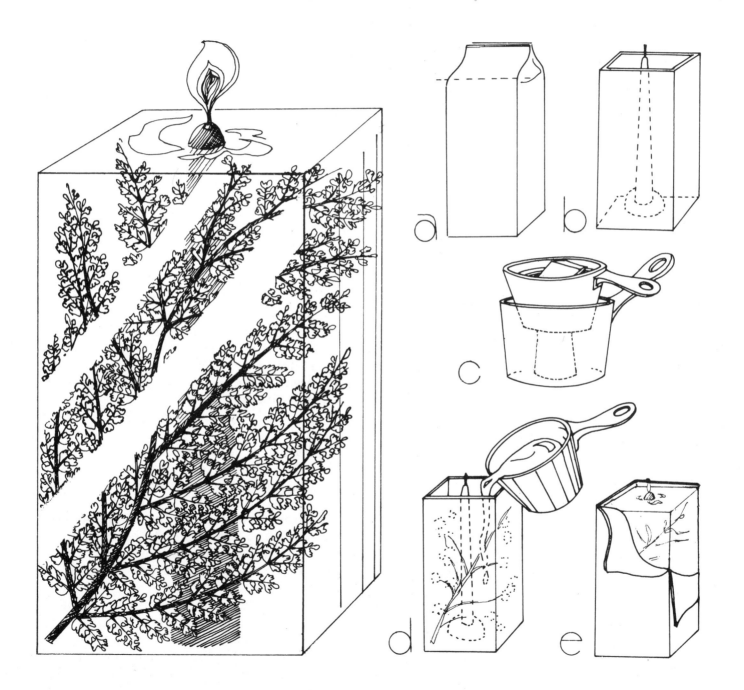

Wax Leaf Ropes

In ancient times, men frequently wore a bit of nature around their heads. If you look at pictures of famous men of the Roman Empire, you will see many of them wearing wreaths of golden leaves. This meant they had special power in the country. Leaf wreaths are also worn today as signs of peace and love. Necklaces, too, can be made like wreaths and spray-painted many different colors. You can make a leaf rope that can be worn about your head as a wreath, or used as a necklace.

Things You Need

paraffin (canning wax)
2 saucepans, one larger than the other
small tin can
newspaper
small tree or bush leaves
waxed paper
needle and thread
small tube macaroni

Let's Begin

**1. Melt wax as explained in *Fern Candle*, page 50.
**2. Remove the pot with the melted wax and place it on the newspaper.
**3. Holding a leaf by its stem, dip it completely into the melted wax. Repeat with all the leaves.
  4. Place the waxed leaves on a sheet of waxed paper.
**5. Thread a needle with sewing thread.
  6. When the leaves have hardened to the touch but are still warm, "thread" them. To do this, pass the threaded needle through the front of the leaf near the top and back through to the front near the bottom, see illustration.
  7. Thread a tube macaroni between each leaf. Continue the alternate stringing of leaves and macaroni until you have a rope.
  8. Tie the ends of the thread together when the rope is as long as you want it.

Placemats and Coasters

Now is your chance to use nature to decorate your dinner table. You can design a set of placemats and coasters you will be proud to sit down to. Find the prettiest leaves you can. Gather all sizes and shapes. This craft would make a great gift for your relatives when you go visiting.

Things You Need

scissors
heavy white drawing paper or colored construction paper
liquid white glue
large tree leaves
waxed paper
heavy books
paintbrush
varnish or liquid plastic finish, available in hardware or art supply stores.

Let's Begin

PLACEMATS
1. Cut heavy paper into rectangles that are large enough to hold a plate and tableware.
2. Squeeze liquid white glue around the entire underneath or veined sides of the leaves, Fig. a.
3. Glue the leaves onto the paper in arrangements that please you, see illustration for an example.
4. Place a piece of waxed paper over the glued leaves.
5. Stack the books over the waxed paper.
6. When the leaves have dried, carefully peel away the waxed paper.
**7. Brush a coating of varnish or plastic finish on to the placemats covering the leaves thoroughly.
**8. When the first coating has dried, give the mats a second coating.
**9. When the second coating has dried, give the mats a third and final coating.

COASTERS
1. Cut heavy paper into square pieces somewhat larger than individual leaves.
2. Using liquid white glue, glue the leaves onto the paper, Fig. b. Be sure to glue them veined side down.
3. When the leaves are dry, cut them from the paper following their outlines, Fig. c.
4. Follow the same directions to finish the coasters as you did the placemats.

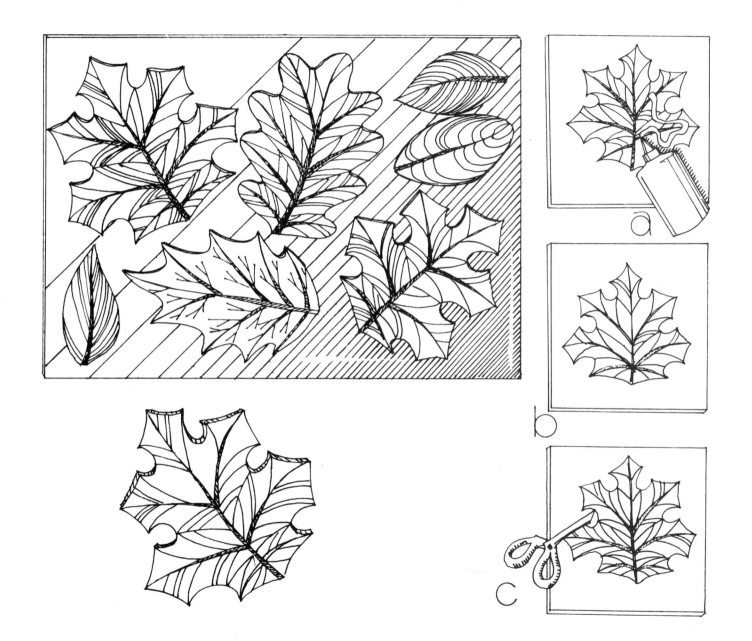

a

b

c

Glycerin Leaves

If you want to preserve a beautiful branch of leaves, this craft is for you. Glycerin—a colorless, odorless syrup that is very sweet—will do the trick. It comes from fats and oils, and is one of the by-products of soapmaking. After being treated with the glycerin, the leaves you collect become stiff, and won't disintegrate or fade. Depending upon the season and where you live, you may use green leaves or leaves that have just turned colors.

Things You Need

small branch with leaves, either green or just
  turning colors
newspaper
hammer
large jar
glycerin (available at drugstores)
scissors
colored construction paper
tall fruit drink can
colored felt-tipped markers or crayons
tape

Let's Begin

1. Place the branch on several layers of newspaper.
**2. With the hammer, tap the end of the stem until it is slightly crushed and feels soft, Fig. a.
3. In the jar, mix one part glycerin to two parts water.
4. Place the pounded end of the branch into the glycerin mixture. Leave the branch in the glycerin for two weeks, by which time the leaves should be preserved. They will have gotten thicker to the touch, and their color will have changed slightly.
5. Cut a piece of colored construction paper as high as the fruit drink can and long enough to wrap all the way around it.
6. Draw a design along the top length of the paper with colored felt-tipped markers or crayons, see illustration.
7. Tape the paper around the can, Fig. b.
8. Display the leaves in the can.

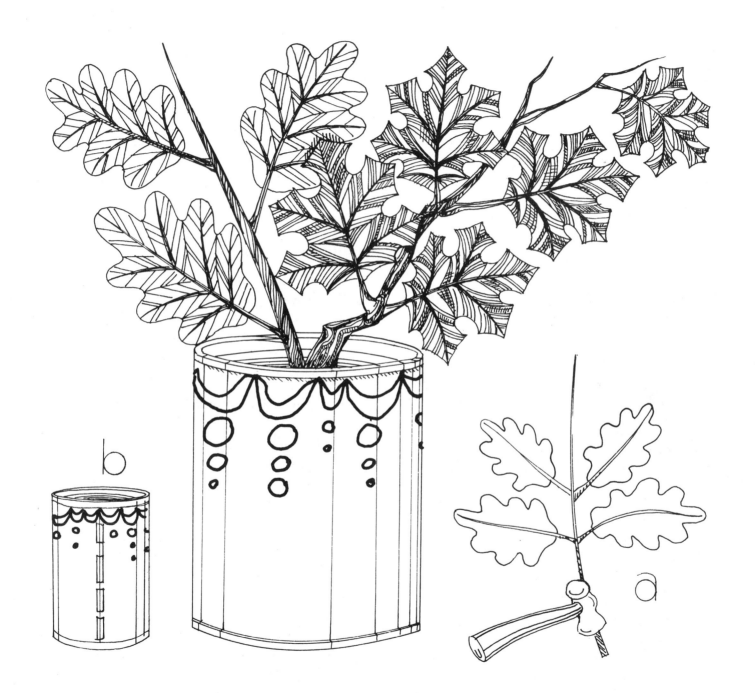

Lucky Clover Bookmark

"I'm looking over a four-leaf clover" is a line from a song composed many years ago. Four-leaf clovers are supposed to bring good luck and the song celebrates the discovery of one. Have you ever found a four-leaf clover? If you look long and hard, you may be able to locate some. In fact, you might well find clovers with five, six, seven, eight, even eleven leaves. Although most clover has only three leaves, clover with more than three leaves are often unearthed.

Although it would be nice to use a four-leaf clover for this craft, the more common three-leaf variety will do very well indeed. The bookmark you make with one will be lucky in that it will help prevent you from losing your place when you stop your reading.

Things You Need

clover, preferably four-leaf, but any kind will do
typewriter paper
heavy book
colored construction paper
liquid white glue
paper cup
paintbrush

Let's Begin

1. Put the clover between two sheets of typewriter paper. Press between the pages of a heavy book.
2. In a few days, check to see if the clover has dried. When it has, take it from between the pressing paper.
3. Cut a strip of colored construction paper a little longer than the book for which you are making the bookmark.
4. Pour a little white glue into a paper cup.
5. Paint the back of the clover with a thin coating of glue.
6. Carefully pick up the glued clover and place it on one end of the paper strip, see illustration. When the clover dries, your bookmark is ready for use.

Twigs
are presents
from a tree

Twigs are presents from a tree

Some of the most exciting crafts you can make come from things that grow right in your own back yard. They come from those huge growing things called trees. If you live in a big city, you may not see too many trees. You may have to travel to the country, or to a park to be really close to one. You really shouldn't have to look too far, however. Almost every part of the world has some trees growing on it. The only exceptions are the desert and the icy polar areas.

Making things from trees has always been important—not only to man, but to animals as well. Many animals use trees for building their homes. Birds make nests from small twigs. Beavers cut down trees to build dams across streams. Even chimpanzees use twigs as a tool to get termites out of termite holes.

The chimp puts a twig in the termite hole, and the termites cling to it. When the twig is taken out of the hole, the chimp has a tasty snack. It is interesting to think that people have copied the habits of animals and are today still building homes from wood cut from trees.

Unlike the chimp, we will use twigs for some good craftwork. Whenever you are near a tree and see some dead branches lying beneath it, collect them for the wood projects in this chapter. Remove the twigs, and stack them according to size. You will need very skinny twigs as well as fat ones. A twig hunt can be a lot of fun, but always remember not to take branches that are alive and have green leaves on them. There are plenty of "twig presents" under the trees to make the crafts which follow.

61

Charm Mobile

Do you know what a mobile is? It is a collection of objects that hang from another object, much bigger in size. This construction doesn't sound too exciting in itself. What is needed to make it more interesting is a light gust of wind. When wind passes through the hanging objects, they sway gracefully in all directions. They move, or become mobile.

You can gather a collection of your favorite things to make a mobile, or begin by using the objects suggested below. In either case, you will have a lot of fun making and watching this "action" toy.

Things You Need

scissors
colored construction paper
paper punch
colored felt-tipped markers or crayons
macaroni, sequins, stick-on paper stars, glitter
liquid white glue
string or yarn
small branch without leaves

Let's Begin

1. Cut different shapes from colored construction paper such as circles, stars, hearts, and triangles.
2. Punch a hole near the top of each paper shape with a paper punch.
3. Decorate the shapes with designs using crayons or colored felt-tipped markers, stick-on paper stars, or by adding macaroni and sequins with liquid white glue.
4. Tie one end of a length of string or yarn through the hole of each decorated shape.
5. Tie the other end of the string or yarn to an arm of the branch.
6. Tie a long length of yarn or string to both ends of the branch for hanging, see illustration.
7. Hang the mobile in your room in an open place so the charms may move freely.

Gumdrop Tree

Some of the strangest-looking things grow on trees. If you read some of your favorite stories, you learn that lollipops, ice cream cones, and even money can be found hanging in the forest. Nature is filled with surprises, but of a different kind than you sometimes read about. What you will find in the woods is a handful of acorns, a tasty apple, or a spindly pine cone. Only you can make a lollipop tree, or maybe a gumdrop tree. If you read on, you will soon have one growing in your own room.

Things You Need

ice-cream stick or spoon
plaster of paris
paper cup
small can
small branch without leaves
scissors
colored construction paper
tape
gumdrops or other candy
cellophane or plastic wrap
string or cord

Let's Begin

1. Using an ice-cream stick or a small spoon, mix water and plaster of paris in a paper cup until it has the consistency of heavy cream. Add water carefully at first to the plaster, mixing all the while; you don't want to add too much water too quickly.
2. Pour the plaster mixture into the can. Fill it halfway.
3. Wait a few minutes, and then push the end of the branch into the plaster in the can.
4. If the branch does not stand by itself in the plaster, hold it until the plaster sets enough for it to do so.
5. Cut a piece of colored construction paper as high as the can and long enough to wrap around it.
6. Wrap the paper around the can and tape it in place.
7. Stand a gumdrop on a piece of cellophane or plastic wrap that has been cut about three times larger than the gumdrop, Fig. a.
8. Bring the ends of the wrap over the top of the gumdrop, Fig. b.
9. Tie the wrap closed with a piece of string or cord, Fig. c.
10. After the plaster has hardened, tie the gumdrops to the branches of the tree.

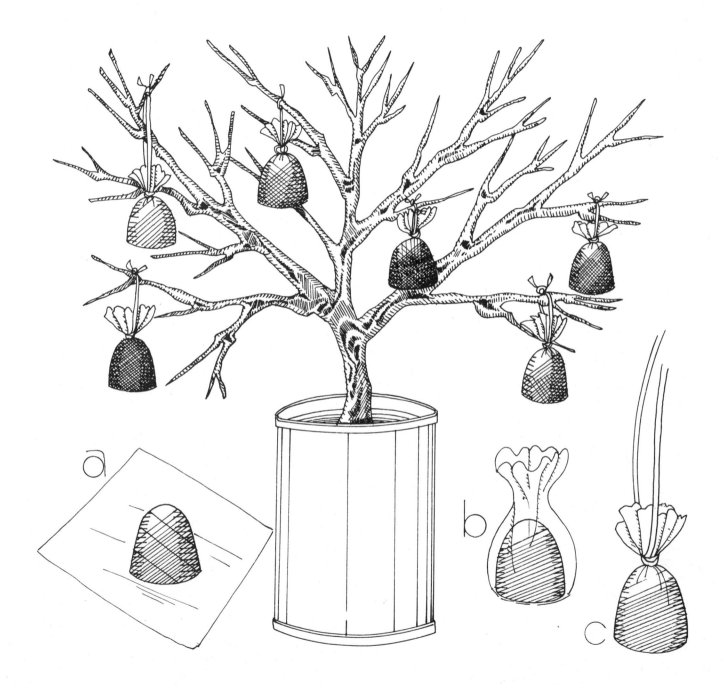

Tomahawk

When you think of the American Indian, many things may come to mind. He was one of the greatest woodsmen living in any country at any time in history. He made all of his own clothing, built his home, hunted his food, and made all of the tools he needed to live. One of the tools that was and still is today very important to him is the tomahawk. It was used as a weapon in wartime, and during peacetime it had a hundred-and-one uses. If you enjoy thinking about the American Indian and his way of life, then you may well want a tomahawk of your own.

Things You Need

thick twig
rectangular sponge
thick cord
scissors

Let's Begin

1. Find a thick twig that feels right in your hand for a tomahawk handle, see illustration.
2. Lay a rectangular sponge over the twig near one end.
3. Slip a thick cord under the twig at the bottom of the sponge, Fig. a.
4. Cross the ends of the cord over the sponge, Fig. b.
5. Bring the ends of the cord back under the end of the twig, Fig. c.
6. Pull the ends tightly on the underside of the twig and knot.
7. Cut away the excess ends of the cord.

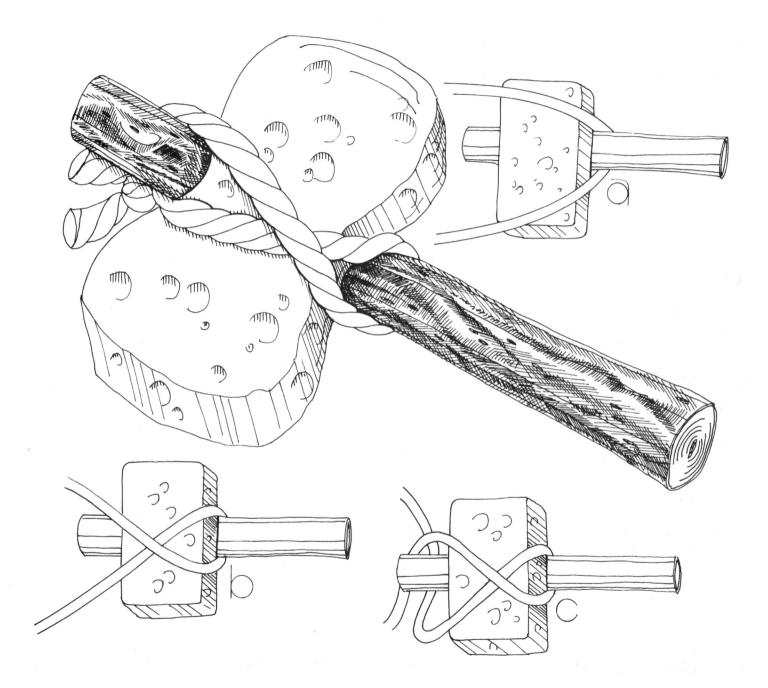

Eye of God

The Eye of God is an interesting craft that comes from Mexico. It is made with two twigs and different colored yarn. Two twigs are crossed and yarn is tied around them. If you use several colors, it will look like a big eye. This is how it got its name.

Things You Need

2 thickish twigs, one longer than the other
liquid white glue
colored yarn
macaroni or beads with large holes

Let's Begin

1. Make a cross with the twigs. That is, cross the smaller twig over the larger near the top of the larger.
2. Using liquid white glue, glue the two twigs together.
3. When the glue has dried, tie the end of a length of colored yarn around the point where the twigs cross on the back side of the cross, Fig. a.
4. Bring the yarn over arm 1 of the cross, down and then under it, Figs. b and c.
5. Bring the yarn behind arm 2. Bring the yarn over arm 2 of the cross, around and over, then behind it, Fig. d.
6. Bring the yarn down behind arm 3 of the cross, around and over, then behind it, Fig. e.
7. Bring the yarn behind arm 4 of the cross, around and over, then behind it, Fig. f.
8. You have now connected the four arms of the crossed twigs by wrapping the yarn around each arm in exactly the same way.
9. Repeat the procedure, doing four more yarn windings.
10. Continue to wrap the yarn around the cross, always moving outward along the arms. (You can use different colored yarns as you wind, or you can thread beads or tube macaroni onto the yarn).
11. Leave a little bit of wood visible at the top and on the sides of the arms. Let more wood show at the bottom.
12. Glue the end of the yarn to the back side of the Eye of God.

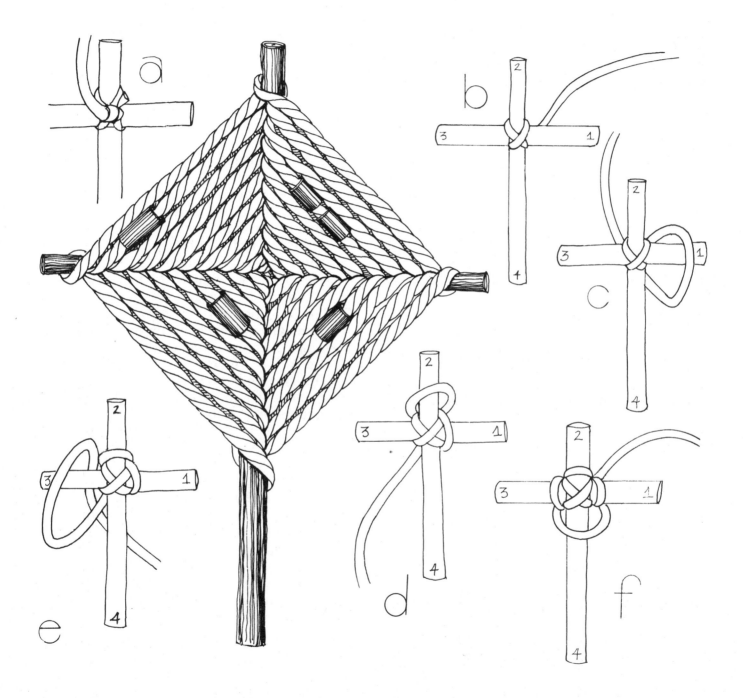

Picture Frame

If you would like to bring the adventure of the woods into your room, do it by framing some of your favorite outdoor pictures. If you don't have any, get some from magazines. Cut out pictures that interest you, and make your own frames. All you need is four twigs. No matter how big or how small your picture may be, you can make a frame to fit it.

Things You Need

4 twigs all the same size, or 2 of one size and 2
   of another.
waxed paper
liquid white glue
thick cord
scissors
colored construction paper
ruler
pencil
tape

Let's Begin

1. Lay two of the same-sized twigs a distance apart on a sheet of waxed paper.
2. Lay the other two twigs across the first two.
3. Arrange the four twigs so that the ends of each stick out a little from the square, Fig. a.
4. Glue the twigs at the points where they cross, using the liquid white glue.
5. Let the frame dry overnight.
6. Tie an Indian knot around the twigs at each of the four corners of the frame. To make the Indian knot, first run the cord where two twigs meet from corner to opposite corner on what will be the underside of the frame, Fig. b.
7. The two ends of the cord will meet. Twist them around each other as if you were making an everyday knot on the front of the frame, Fig. c.
8. The two ends now go to the back of the frame, each end around one of the untied corners, Fig. d, back view.
9. Tie the ends together in a tight knot, Fig. e.
10. Cut a piece of colored construction paper to fit perfectly in the frame.
11. Use a ruler to draw a window in the center of the paper. There should be an equal amount of paper border on all sides of the window, Fig. f.
12. Cut out the window.
13. Tape a picture into the window. Make sure the picture is centered.
14. Glue the paper with the picture to the back of the frame.

a

b

c

d

e

f

Tepee

The American Indian built a home that was comparatively simple to make. All he had to do was to chop down some tall young trees, cut off all branches, tie the narrow ends of the trees together, and stand the framework up. Around this he wrapped skins or bark from trees. In a matter of hours, he could construct a home for himself and his family.

You may not have room in your home for a large tepee, but you can learn the skills of the Indians by making a smaller version. If you make enough tepees, you can have a whole Indian nation.

Things You Need

scissors
small dish
pencil
cardboard
6 twigs
cord
liquid white glue
colored construction paper
colored felt-tipped markers or crayons
tape

Let's Begin

1. Cut a circle from the cardboard. Use the small dish to trace the circle.
**2. Cut out six small equally spaced holes around the outer edge, Fig. a.
**3. Saw the twigs so that they are equal in size (or maybe you can find six twigs of the same size).
4. Push one end of each of the twigs a little bit through the holes in the cardboard so that the little feet are the same length, Fig. b.
5. Gather all the twigs at the top and tie them together with a piece of cord, Fig. c. Add a dab of glue to the knot.
6. With crayons or colored felt-tipped markers, draw Indian designs on a long piece of colored construction paper that is as tall as the tepee frame and will fit around it. Tape pieces of construction paper together if you need a very long piece.
7. Wrap the paper around the tepee's frame, and tape the ends together, Fig. d.
8. Trim the bottom of the paper to the height of the inside cardboard circle, Fig. e.
9. Cut a triangular door out of the bottom edge of the paper cover.

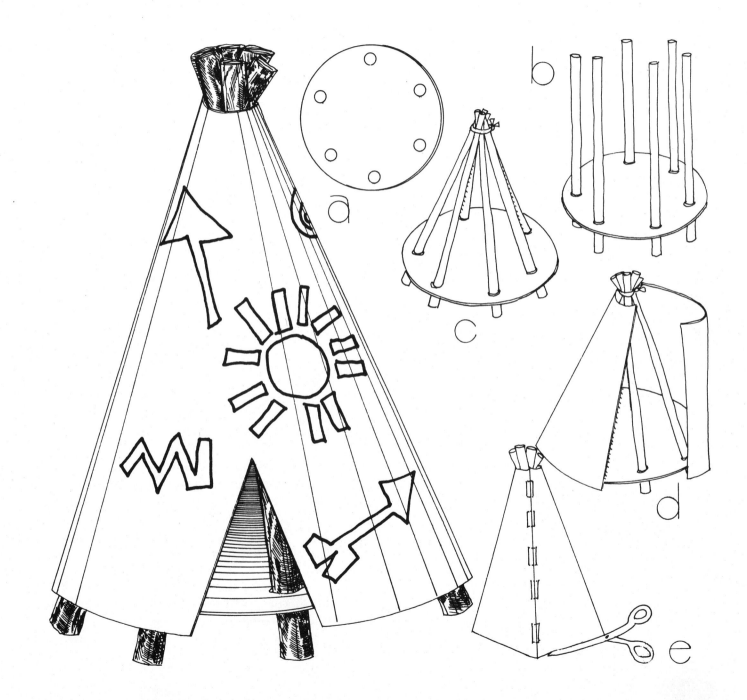

a

b

c

d

e

Log Cabin

When the first settlers came to America they built wooden homes. Not having the tools they needed with them, they devised a simple means of construction using logs to build their cabins. These structures had only one room with a fireplace. Everything was done in this one room. There are very few original log cabins still standing, but you can see something of what they looked like when you build one yourself. You can imagine how difficult it was to live in America many hundreds of years ago!

Things You Need

at least 14 twigs of the same thickness
saw
waxed paper
liquid white glue
colored construction paper
scissors
colored felt-tipped markers or crayons.

Let's Begin

****1. Saw all the twigs to the same length.
2. Place two twigs (group Number 1 in Fig. a) on a sheet of waxed paper a little away from each other, Fig. a.
3. Place two more twigs (Number 2) over the first two twigs. Arrange the twigs to look as they do in Fig. b.
4. Once the four twigs are in place, lift up one Number 2 twig and squeeze a dab of liquid white glue on the places where it touches the Number 1 twigs.
5. Glue the twig carefully in place on the Number 1 twigs.
6. Do the same with the other Number 2 twig, Fig. b.
7. Let the four twigs dry completely.
8. When dry, glue two more Number 1 twigs over the glued frame.
9. Follow with two more Number 2 twigs.
10. Keep building up twigs, letting each group of four dry before you add four more.
11. Make the roof out of a piece of colored construction paper folded in half. Cut the paper to fit neatly across the top of the cabin.
12. Draw a shingle design onto the roof with crayons or colored felt-tipped markers.
13. Cut a strip of colored construction paper to make a chimney.
14. Fold the strip in half and cut the ends of the strip into a point, Fig. c. Draw a brick design on it.
15. Cut two small slits in the roof, Fig. d.
16. Push the points of the chimney into the slits in the roof.
17. Glue the roof to the log cabin and your log cabin is finished.

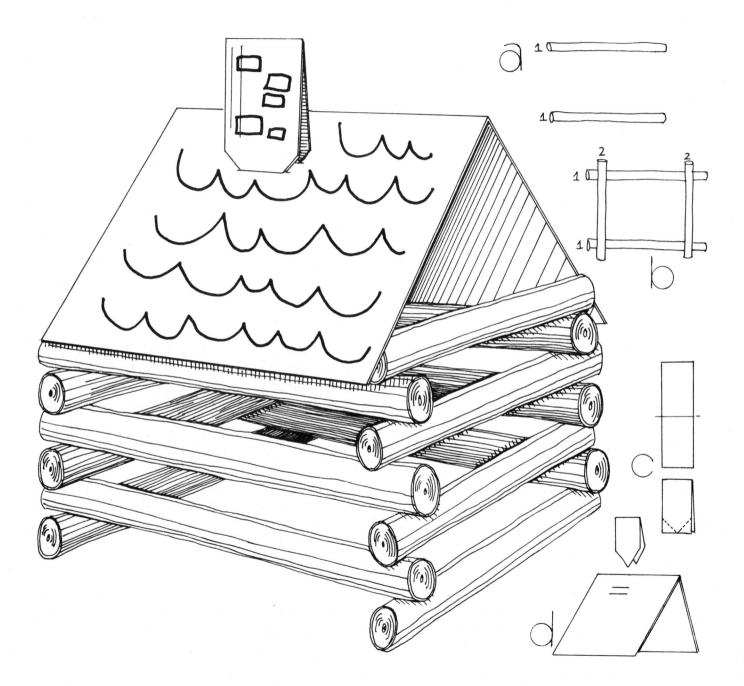

a

b

c

d

Bird Feeder

One important thing you and nature's feathered friends have in common, as you might well guess, is the need for food. You can help feed them by hanging one of these bird feeders outside your window, and putting birdseed in it.

Things You Need

cardboard or oaktag
scissors
pencil
ruler
liquid white glue
twigs
saw
waxed paper
cord

Let's Begin

1. Cut the cardboard into two triangles of equal size. Make the sides of the triangles longer than the bottom.
2. Using a pencil and ruler, draw a line down the three sides of each triangle a little way in from the edges, see dotted line in Fig. a.
3. Cut a slit from the points of the triangles to the points where the pencil lines cross. See the three heavy lines in Fig. a.
4. Cut out a triangular shape from the bottom center of each triangle, see shaded area in Fig. a.
5. Make folds along all the pencil lines.
6. Overlap the cut paper points on each corner and glue them down. This gives edges to the triangles, Fig. b.
**7. Saw all but three of the twigs to the same size. These three should be longer.
8. On a piece of waxed paper, lay out the right number of twigs to fit as a floor between the two bottom corners of each triangle. Use a long twig for the center twig of the floor, Fig. c.
9. Squeeze glue between all the twigs.
10. Squeeze glue on the bottom edge of each triangle.
11. Glue each triangle, with the folded sides facing in, across the twigs, Fig. d.
12. Let the glue dry overnight.
13. On a piece of waxed paper, lay out the twigs to fit one side of the feeder. Use a long twig on the top corner, Fig. e.
14. Squeeze liquid white glue between the twigs and on corresponding edges of each triangle. Glue triangles to the twigs, Fig. e. Let dry thoroughly.
15. Repeat the procedure of making a twig side and gluing it to the remaining triangle edges. Make sure that both long twigs are together at the top of the feeder.
16. Tie a length of cord around the two long top twigs for hanging the feeder.

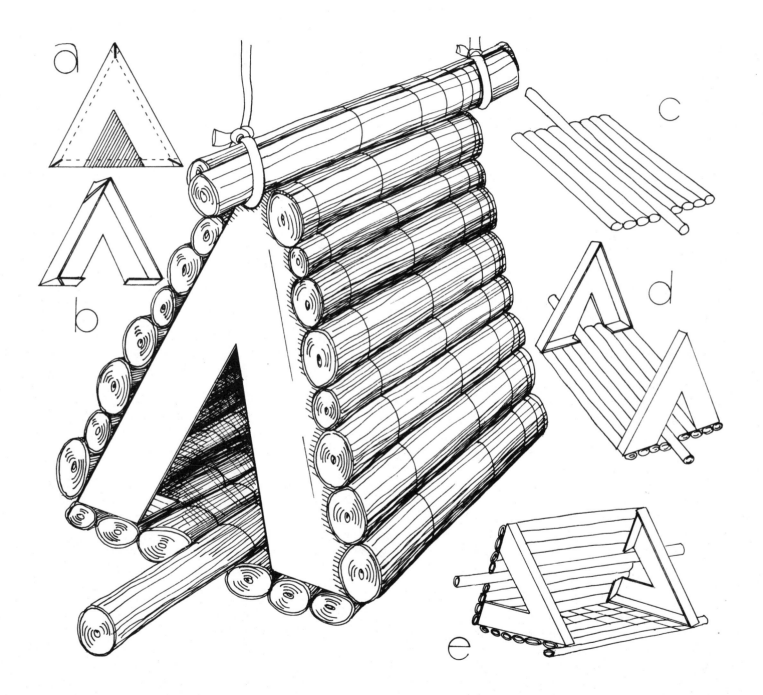

a

b

c

d

e

Fishing Pole and Bow and Arrow

When you think of the hunting tools of the Indians, you probably think first of bows and arrows. When the Indians went fishing they used a long pole with a hook attached to it. These were very useful food-gathering tools indeed. Today's bow and arrow and fishing pole really haven't changed all that much. Why not make some of your own? You will probably enjoy these even more than the kind you buy.

Things You Need

string
long, thin, straight twigs
short twigs
marshmallows
safety pin

Let's Begin

BOW AND ARROW
1. Tie string to both ends of a long, thin, straight twig. Pull it tightly so that the twig bends, see illustration. Don't make your bow too large to handle.
2. Make the arrows from shorter twigs with a marshmallow pushed on one end as an arrowhead.

FISHING POLE
1. Tie a string to one end of a long, thin twig.
2. Tie a safety pin (opened) to the end of the string. (Hope you catch a big one.)

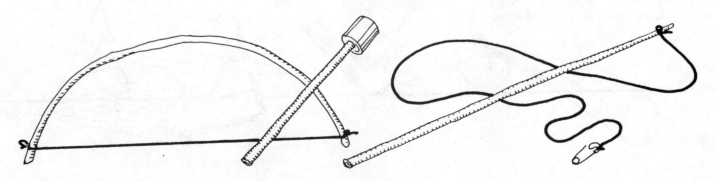

A pine cone
is a nursery
for seeds

A pine cone is a nursery for seeds

A pine cone might be called a nursery for seeds. Seeds stay in this nursery until they are old enough to leave their rooms and fall to the ground to become a giant pine tree. Once this happens, the pine cone goes out of business and falls to the earth. Did you know that cones grow on other trees as well? Spruce, fir, and balsam grow cones. Unless you know the kind of tree you are looking at, you won't know what kind of cone you have.

Animals as well as people use the seeds of pine cones. Both squirrels and people eat the seeds. We call them Indian nuts, because the Indians used them for food. They are very tasty and can be used in cooking. You will not find seeds large enough to eat, so leave them to the squirrels.

The variety of Indian nuts that people eat comes from Europe. They grow in pine cones that are almost one foot long.

Pine cones are good to use in craft projects. Be sure to bring a large paper bag with you on your next journey into the forest, but never pick cones that are still on the trees. They are still alive and have not dropped their seeds. You may use any kind of cone for the crafts. If you can find a part of the forest where many cones have fallen, you should be able to gather enough for all the exciting projects in this chapter.

Wild Bird Feeder

If you live in the country you know that the wild birds are always looking for food. One way to feed them is with the kind of feeder that you put seeds into, and which birds come and perch on. There is another method of feeding these hungry critters. Believe it or not, a large pine cone, seeds, and a jar of peanut butter is all you need (you are not the only person who likes a good peanut butter dinner). Keep the jar of jelly in the house. If the wild birds ever taste peanut butter and jelly together, Mom will have to buy two jars of each—one for you and one for the birds!

Things You Need

cord
large pine cone
spoon
peanut butter
birdseed
waxed paper

Let's Begin

1. Tie the cord to the top petals of the pine cone.
2. Spoon peanut butter between the petals.
3. Place birdseed on the waxed paper.
4. Roll the peanut buttered pine cone in the birdseed.
5. Hang the feeder in a tree.

Feathered Friends

If you look at a pine tree, you will see birds flying in and out. Many birds nest in these trees because they offer good shelter and a nice place to live. You won't mistake pine cones for birds, unless they are decorated with paper wings and faces. You can make these pine cone birds if you follow the directions below. With a little imagination they will look like common birds you have seen in the forest. Collect long, round, and oval pine cones for this craft.

Things You Need

different shaped pine cones
pencil
scissors
colored construction paper
liquid white glue
crayons
string

Let's Begin

HANGING BIRD
1. Choose a long pine cone.
2. Cut two paper wings from colored construction paper and glue them to the sides of the pine cone, see illustration.
3. Cut a strip of paper twice as long as it is wide.
4. Fold the paper in half.
5. Cut out a circle from the folded paper, leav-ing part of the fold uncut, see illustration.
6. Cut a very small slit into the folded side of the circle.
7. Cut a small beak shape from construction paper and push it into the cut slit. Draw an eye on both sides of the beak.
8. Open the paper head slightly, and glue over the wide end of the pine cone.
9. Tie string to a top petal and hang.

TURKEY
1. Lay a round pine cone on its side.
2. Cut several paper feathers from construction paper, see illustration.
3. Draw vein designs on the feathers with crayons.
4. Glue the feathers into the top petals of the pine cone.
5. Cut a head and neck out of construction paper, see illustration. Draw an eye on the head and glue on a red paper circle under the eye for a wattle (the fleshy piece of skin turkeys have under their necks.
6. Glue the head to the bottom of the pine cone.

OWL
1. Stand an oval pine cone on its bottom end.
2. Cut round paper eyes and a beak out of construction paper.
3. Glue the eyes and beak to the top of the pine cone.

Pine Cone Elves

Santa Claus is lucky because he has a group of faithful helpers. These elves help make the toys and load the sled for that all-night sleigh ride. You may or may not believe in Santa's elves, but a collection of these cute creatures would be fun to have.

Things You Need

scissors
cardboard
liquid white glue
small beads or dried beans
small, round pine cones
acorns, large beads, small foam balls
colored felt-tipped markers
yarn
pipe cleaners
colored construction paper
tab from soft-drink can
cotton tufts
stick-on paper stars
toothpick

Let's Begin

1. Cut a circle from the cardboard.
2. Glue two small beads or dried beans to the center of the cardboard circle. These will be feet for the figures.
3. Let the beads or beans dry.
4. Press the top petals of a pine cone on a table to make a flat surface (you will glue the head to this surface).
5. Glue the bottom of the pine cone to the feet on the cardboard circle. Make sure the feet stick out just a little.
6. When the cone has dried on the circle, glue an acorn, large bead, or small foam ball onto the top of the cone for a head.
7. Draw on eyes with felt-tipped markers.
8. Wrap a pipe cleaner around the upper part of the cone for arms.

ANGEL ELF
1. Glue yarn to the head for hair.
2. Make a book out of a folded square of colored construction paper and glue to the hands.
3. Use the tab from a soft-drink can for a halo.

MUSICIAN ELF
1. Make hair out of a strip of colored construction paper cut into a fringe.
2. Make a cone hat out of a circular piece of colored construction paper which is slit to the center and wrapped around itself. Glue the hat to the head.
3. Fold a strip of paper back and forth for an accordion and glue it to the hands.

MAGIC GODMOTHER ELF
1. Glue cotton tufts to the head for hair. Add stick-on paper stars to the hair.
2. Top a toothpick with a stick-on paper star. Glue wand to the pipe cleaner arms.

Cone Flowers

In this chapter the scales of a pine cone are referred to as petals. If you study a pine cone very carefully it looks very much like a flower made of wood. Just like a flower, a pine cone has petals that are closed while it is growing. When the cones are fully grown, they open their petals and spread their seeds so that new plants can grow. Collect an assortment of pine cones and you can create a garland of pretty cone flowers.

Things You Need

pipe cleaners
medium-sized round pine cones
scissors
colored construction paper
drinking straws
liquid white glue

Let's Begin

1. Wrap a pipe cleaner around the last ring of petals at the bottom of a pine cone. Twist ends together leaving one end of the pipe cleaner longer than the other end, Fig. a.
2. Cut a circle from colored construction paper twice as large as the bottom of a pine cone.
3. Cut circular petal shapes around the edge of the circle and make a small hole in the middle, Fig. b.
4. Push the longer end of the pipe cleaner through the center of the paper petals, Fig. c.
5. Twist the end of the pipe cleaner tightly around the top of a drinking straw.
6. Add a dab of liquid white glue where the pipe cleaner is wrapped around the straw. Let dry overnight.
7. Cut out green construction paper leaves and glue to straw stems.

Candle Holder

Candles are becoming more popular each and every day. You may have a decorative or funny candle somewhere in your room or elsewhere in your home. There is a special fascination about candles. It is fun to watch the flame dance with its favorite partner, the soft breeze that makes it flicker in all directions. The flame moves to every whisper and vibration in the room. If you talk to it, it seems to be talking back to you.

If you enjoy candles, then you will need a safe candle holder. You can make one with pine cones and a tin can. It can be used in your room for your enjoyment, or placed on the dining room table during the holiday season. Enjoying candles can be fun, but you must be extra careful with them. Candles involve fire, and you know how dangerous that can be. When you light a candle, always be careful.

Things You Need

yarn
small, round pine cones
tin can with label removed (soak off with hot
    water)
red poster paint or paper
paintbrush
ribbon
play clay (or any non-hardening clay)
candle

Let's Begin

1. Tie two pieces of yarn together around the last ring of petals at the bottom of each pine cone, Fig. a. Be sure each side has a length of yarn hanging from it.
2. Tie two pine cones together by knotting one length of yarn of one pine cone to another length of yarn on a second pine cone, Fig. b.
3. Continue tying pine cones together to form a string of pine cones long enough to fit around the tin can.
4. Paint the tin can with red poster paint or cover with red paper.
5. Arrange the cones around the bottom of the can, see illustration.
6. Tie a ribbon around the can and into a bow.
7. Stick a large ball of play clay onto the bottom of the tin can.
8. Push a candle into the clay.

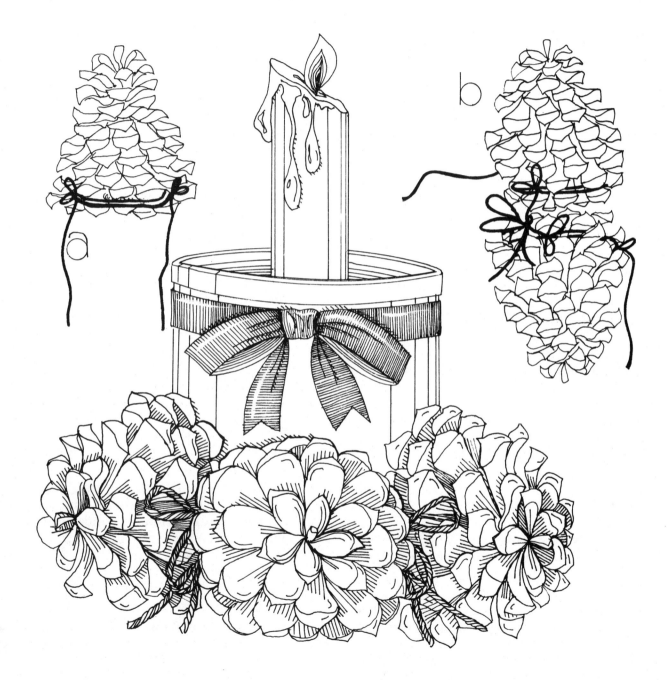

Door Wreath

When you are visiting friends and relatives at Christmas time, the first thing you notice is the wreath on the door. You can buy a pretty wreath at the store, but maybe this year you and your family can make one with pine cones. You may just have the most spectacular Christmas wreath in your neighborhood this holiday season.

Things You Need

pipe cleaners
small, round pine cones
pencil
large sheet of cardboard
compass or large plate and small plate
scissors
green poster paint
paintbrush
paper punch
red construction paper
string

Let's Begin

1. Wrap a pipe cleaner around the last ring of petals on the bottom of each pine cone and twist the ends together, leaving one end longer than the other, Fig. a.
2. Draw a large circle on the sheet of cardboard with a compass opened as wide as it will go or trace around a large plate.
3. Draw a smaller circle in the center of the larger circle with the compass or small plate.
**4. Cut out the larger circle from the cardboard.
**5. Cut out the smaller inner circle, Fig. b.
6. Paint the cardboard wreath shape with the green poster paint.
7. Punch a hole in the center of the rim, green side facing you, Fig. c.
8. Take one of the prepared pine cones and slip the end of the pipe cleaner through the punched hole.
9. Place a second pine cone next to the first cone on the circle. Mark, with a pencil, the center point where the second pine cone falls on the wreath.
10. Punch a hole through this pencil point.
11. Push the end of the pipe cleaner of the second cone through the second hole.
12. Twist the pipe cleaner ends of the first and second cone together on the underside of the wreath.
13. Continue marking points, punching holes, inserting pine cones, and twisting together pipe cleaner ends until the wreath is covered with cones.
14. Cut a bow from paper, Fig. d.
15. Punch two holes in the middle of the bow.
16. Put a pipe cleaner through the two holes.
17. Twist the pipe cleaner ends of the bow around a pine cone on the wreath.
18. Wrap the string around the top cone—and hang on a door.

b

a

d

c

Tall Tree

Pine cones grow on pine trees, but did you ever see a tree with just pine cones instead of branches? Of course you haven't. But you can make one very easily. Gather many small, round pine cones that are about the same size and shape. If you arrange them according to the directions, a beautiful pine cone tree will be the result. Place this tree in your bedroom, or maybe Mom can use it as a centerpiece for the dining room table.

Things You Need

large sheet of cardboard
compass or large plate
pencil
scissors
liquid white glue
small, round pine cones
white drawing paper
tape
ribbons

Let's Begin

1. Draw a large circle on the cardboard with a compass or trace around a large plate.
**2. Cut out the circle with the scissors.
3. Glue pine cones along the rim of the circle, Fig. a.
4. When the glue has dried, roll a piece of heavyweight paper into a cone that will fit into the ring of pine cones, Fig. b.
5. Tape the cone together.
6. Trim the bottom edge of the cone so that it will stand straight in the ring of pine cones.
7. Glue a second ring of pine cones on top of the first ring, placing each new cone between two previously attached cones. Glue cones to cones, pressing new cones closely against the paper cone.
8. Build rings of pine cones to the top of the paper cone. Each new ring should rest on the previously glued ring. The taller the paper cone, the taller your tree will be.
9. Tie lengths of ribbon into bows.
10. Glue ribbon bows onto the tree.

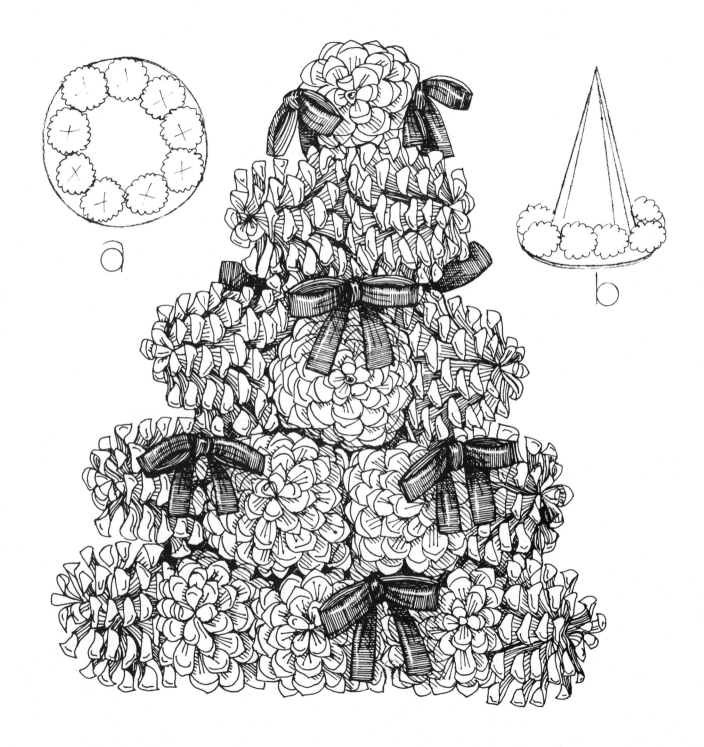

a

b

Small Christmas Tree

Christmas has its own special feeling. One of the things that creates that feeling is the annual shopping for the Christmas tree. You want one that is full so that it can be completely covered with decorations and lights.

It's too bad that Christmas can't be around all year long. The tree starts to turn yellow, and that is a sign that the holidays are over. You can keep a touch of Christmas all year long, however, by making a pine cone Christmas tree. Choose a large pine cone, and decorate it as you do a Christmas tree. Take it out whenever you get the Christmas feeling, even if it's during the hot summer months.

Things You Need

liquid white glue
paper cup
paintbrush
large, well-formed pine cone
glitter or plastic snow
tiny glass balls or beads
scissors
yellow or gold stick-on paper stars

Let's Begin

1. Pour a little liquid white glue into a paper cup.
2. Paint the glue on all the petal tips of the pine cone.
3. Sprinkle glitter or plastic snow on all glued petals.
4. Shake off the excess glitter or snow.
5. Let the pine cone dry.
6. Glue tiny balls or beads wherever you wish on the pine cone. Some beads may be wedged between the petals.
7. Cut out shapes like stars and hearts from colored paper and glue them to the tree.
8. Attach a stick-on paper star to the top of the pine cone tree.

Beans, nuts, and seeds before they grow up

Beans, nuts, and seeds before they grow up

You learned from the last chapter that Indian nuts live and grow in pine cones. All seeds grow inside some kind of "home." Many of these homes are your favorite things to eat—fruits like watermelon. Beans and nuts are also seeds. The largest of all seeds is that tropical delight, the coconut. The shell of the coconut houses and protects the seed or meat within. Beans, seeds and nuts have one thing in common. If you plant them in the ground and give them proper care, they will grow into the living plants themselves. In this chapter, however, you will be making exciting crafts with seeds, not planting them.

There are many wonderful projects to make with seeds, things like bean bags, cantaloupe seed necklaces, and a fleet of walnut shell ships. As you look through this chapter, make a list of the different kinds of seeds you will need, and start collecting them. (Save watermelon seeds instead of spitting them into the garbage can or at your friends!) Let all seeds dry and place them in jars. You will enjoy making seed crafts, not to mention the fringe benefits derived from eating that great cold slice of melon or those delicious walnut meats!

Walnut Ships

One of the most adventurous journeys you could take would be on a sailing ship. Imagine being the captain of a three-masted clipper riding the waves to unknown places. Very few people are lucky enough to travel this way. If you've always wanted this type of life, start learning all about ships and how they are built. Or make your own fleet with walnut shells, toothpicks, and paper. Now you can be the captain of a sailboat, a three-masted clipper, and a pirate ship. All are seaworthy, and will give you hours of fun on the high seas of your bathtub.

Things You Need

play clay (any non-hardening clay)
walnut-shell halves
scissors
colored construction paper
liquid white glue
toothpicks
colored felt-tipped markers or crayons

Let's Begin

1. Press small balls of clay into walnut-shell halves. Continue by following the directions for one or more of the ships described below.

SAILBOAT
1. Cut a triangular sail from the colored construction paper. Don't make the sail larger than toothpick size.
2. Using liquid white glue, glue the sail to a toothpick. Leave enough toothpick at the bottom to push into the clay, see illustration.
3. Let the sail dry.

CLIPPER SHIP
1. Cut three squares from colored construction paper. Make one a little smaller than the other two.
2. Draw a design—like the cross in the illustration—on the smaller square with colored felt-tipped markers or crayons.
3. Push toothpicks through the tops and bottoms of each sail, see illustration. Leave enough toothpick mast at the bottom to push into the clay.
4. Cut an anchor from colored construction paper and glue it to the side of the shell.

PIRATE SHIP
1. Cut two rectangles from the colored construction paper, one larger than the other.
2. Decorate the larger rectangle with a pirate's skull and crossbones, see illustration.
3. Using liquid white glue, glue the sails, with the larger one on the bottom, to the toothpick, see illustration.
4. Let the sails dry. Push toothpick into the shell.

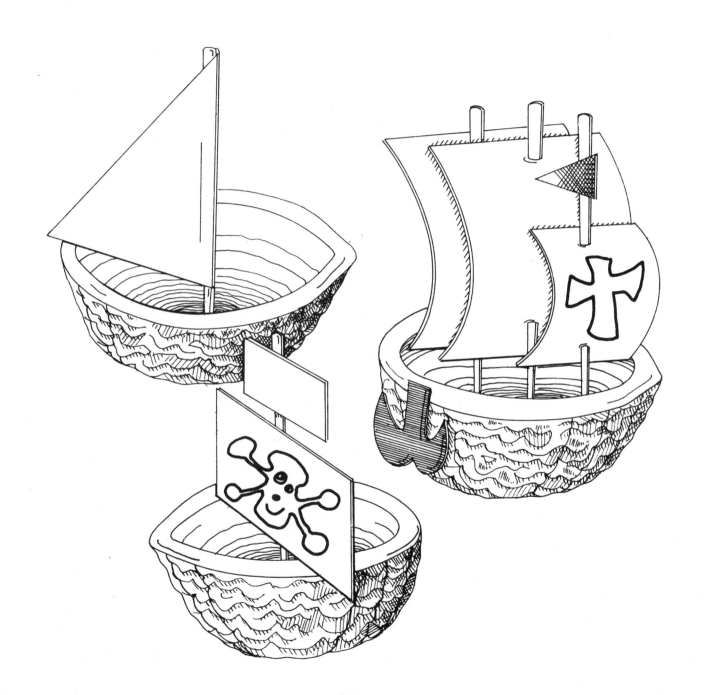

Walnut Animals

There are certain animal pets that you can have in your house. Others, you'll just have to make. Here is the opportunity to create a zoo of animals for your bedroom. After you have finished making the four creatures in this project, you can start designing many more on your own for your collection.

Things You Need

walnut-shell halves
colored construction paper
pencil
scissors
liquid white glue
poster paints or colored felt-tipped markers
paintbrush
pipe cleaners or cord

Let's Begin

1. Place the flat side of a walnut-shell half on a piece of colored construction paper.
2. Trace the outline of the shell with a pencil, Fig. a.
3. Cut out along the shell's outline.
4. Squirt liquid white glue onto the rim of the shell, Fig. b.
5. Place the paper cutout on the glue and make one or more of the animals described below.

WHALE
1. Color the shell gray or blue with poster paint or a colored felt-tipped marker.
2. Cut out a tail from blue construction paper, see illustration.
3. Using liquid white glue, glue the tail to the underside of the shell, see illustration.
4. Cut out two white construction paper eyes and a blue fringe of spouting water and glue them to the shell.

PLATYPUS
1. Color the shell brown with poster paint or a colored felt-tipped marker.
2. Cut out feet, tail and nose from orange construction paper, see illustration.
3. Using liquid white glue, glue the parts to the underside of the shell, see illustration.

TURTLE
1. Color the shell green with poster paint or a colored felt-tipped marker.
2. Cut out the head, feet and tail from green construction paper, see illustration.
3. Using liquid white glue, glue the parts to the underside of the shell, see illustration.

MOUSE
1. Color the shell gray or white with poster paint or colored felt-tipped markers.
2. Cut out ears from pink construction paper and whiskers and eyes from white.
3. Using liquid white glue, glue the parts to the shell, see illustration.
4. Glue a cord or pipe cleaner tail to the shell.

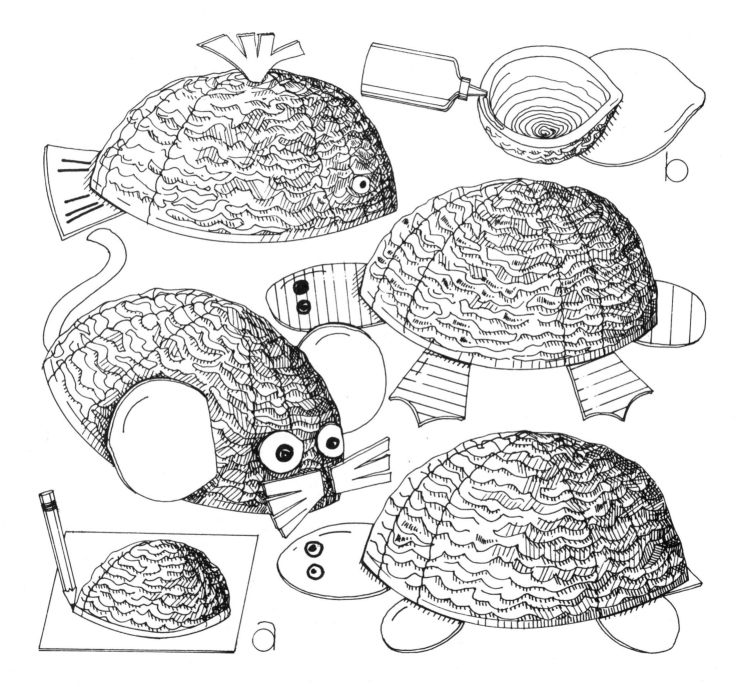

a

b

Walnut Photo Case

If you have any photographs or pictures you would like specially mounted, then you can make a pretty photo case out of walnut shells. Use pictures that are small. (If you don't have photographs, cut pictures from newspapers or magazines.) Once you have selected your favorite pictures, make one or several of these photo cases. They make wonderful gifts for any member of your family, especially those who live far away from you. You can never get tired of seeing the people and things you love so very dearly.

Things You Need

walnut-shell halves
photographs or pictures
pencil
scissors
liquid white glue
felt or fabric

Let's Begin

**1. Divide a walnut very carefully into two perfect halves. Mom or Dad can help by putting the pointed end of a knife into the seam of the back blunt end of the shell to twist it open.

2. Place the flat rim of the shell over the part of the photograph you want to show in your case.

3. Trace around the shell pressing the pencil deep into the photo, Fig. a.

4. Repeat with another photo or picture.

5. Cut out the photos or pictures along the pencil line.

6. Squeeze liquid white glue around the rim of the shells, Fig. b.

7. Place the backs of the cut photos onto the glued shells matching the shapes of photos to shells. Let them dry.

8. When the photos have dried, put the two shells together as they were before the walnut was opened.

9. Cut a small rectangle out of felt or fabric for a hinge.

10. Glue the fabric over both shell halves on one side, Fig. c.

11. Open the case when the fabric hinge has dried.

a

b

c

Acorn Grapes

Most people think that squirrels are the only animals that eat acorns. What you didn't know is that people eat acorns too. The Indians used acorns as snacks, to make a hot drink, and as flour for making bread. Although acorns are very bitter when eaten raw, they lose some of their bitterness when boiled for about two hours. Acorns from white oak trees are sweeter than other kinds. If you are not in the mood for a bowl of roasted acorns, then use these green shelled nuts in art projects, such as acorn grapes.

Things You Need

acorns
cellophane or plastic wrap
scissors
pipe cleaners
green construction paper
paper punch

Let's Begin

1. Place an acorn on a piece of cellophane or plastic wrap and cut the wrap into a square about three times larger than the acorn.
2. Put the acorn in the center of the wrap. The point of the acorn should be facing down with the "little cap" facing up, Fig. a.
3. Bring all of the corners of the wrap up and over the base of the acorn, Fig. b.
4. Twist the wrap ends tightly around the base of the acorn, Fig. c.
5. Twist a pipe cleaner around the twisted wrap leaving one end longer for a stem, Fig. d.
6. Make many acorn grapes in the same way.
7. To make a cluster of acorn grapes, start by twisting two pipe cleaner stems together, Fig. e.
8. Continue to twist together pipe cleaner stems with wrapped acorns.
9. Cut a paper leaf from green construction paper.
10. Punch a hole in the leaf and twist a pipe cleaner into the hole, Fig. f.
11. Tightly twist together the pipe cleaner leaf to the pipe cleaner stems of the grape cluster, see illustration.

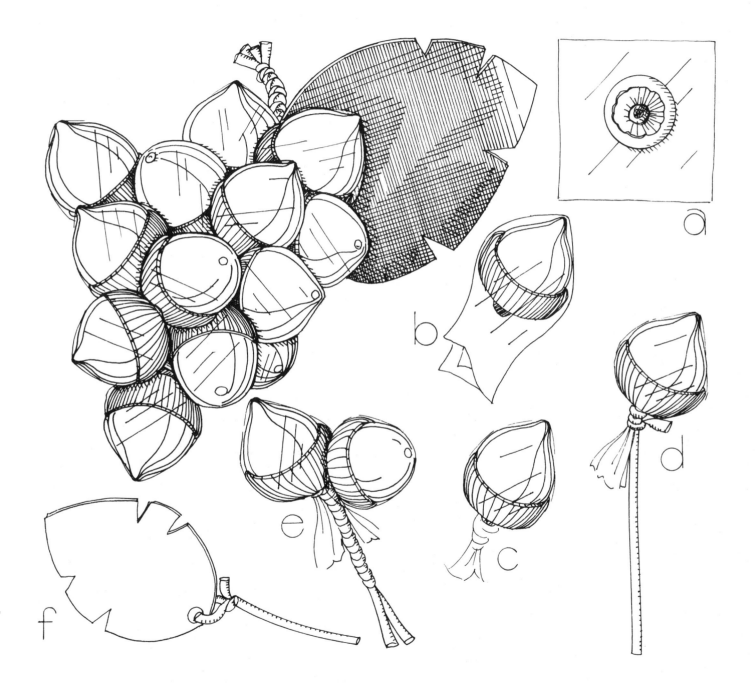

Nut Tree

Autumn is the nut season. Trees that bear nuts are usually ready for harvest during this season. If you walk in the woods in autumn, you will see squirrels and other animals gathering hickory nuts, acorns, and an occasional black walnut. Most of the nuts you buy in the store grow in other parts of the world, however, and very few can be found in the woods near your home. In any case, only one type of nut grows on any tree. But the tree you are going to make contains all of your favorite nuts.

Things You Need

tape
colored construction paper
scissors
waxed paper
liquid white glue
mixed nuts and peanuts, all in their shells

Let's Begin

1. Tape two sheets of construction paper together, one on top of the other.
2. Roll the paper to form a cone, Fig. a.
3. Tape the cone together, Fig. b.
4. Trim the bottom edge of the cone so that the cone stands straight, Fig. c.
5. Place the cone on a sheet of waxed paper.
6. Glue walnuts, or the largest nuts you have, along the bottom of the cone. Squeeze a dab of glue to the side of the nuts and press them in a ring all around the bottom of the cone.
7. Let the nuts dry before you glue on the second ring of nuts.
8. Keep gluing on rings of nuts letting each ring dry before you add the next ring, see illustration.
9. When the tree is complete, carefully peel away the waxed paper.

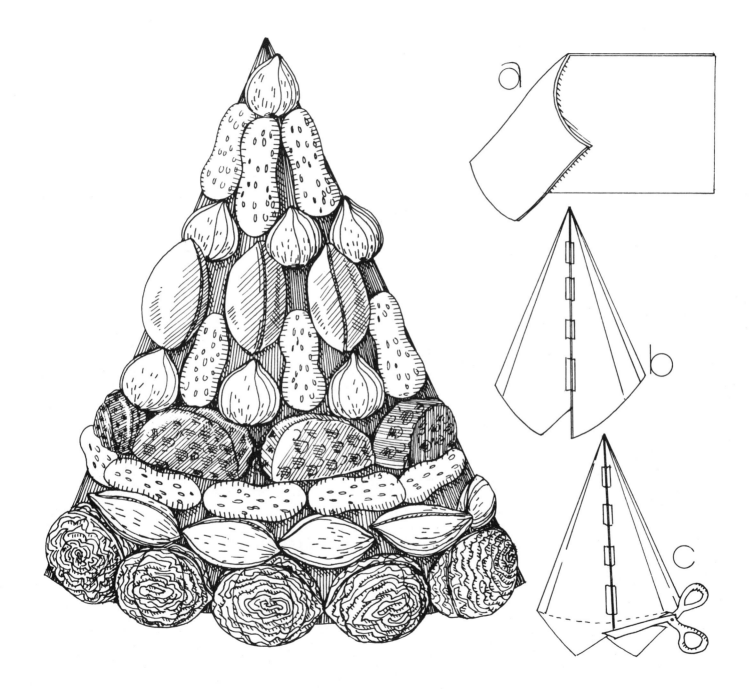

Bean Layering

Dried beans, the kind people use when they make homemade soup, come in many shapes and colors. You know how good they are to eat, but did you know that they can be used in a variety of craft projects? One of the prettiest is bean layering. Mom may store beans in old jars with different beans in each one. Usually you don't want to mix the beans together in a single jar, at least if you want to use them. But there is a beautiful way of mixing different beans to look at. The result is layers of different colors and sizes of beans neatly packed into a jar. It will make a pretty addition to the kitchen or to a special corner in your room.

Things You Need

large jar with a lid

spoon

dried lentils, kidney beans, black-eyed peas, split peas, or any other kind of dried beans

Let's Begin

1. If the jar has a label, place it in water and soak until the paper label slips off. In any case, wash the jar and lid, and dry carefully.
2. Spoon the first kind of bean into the jar to form the first layer, which can be as high as you wish.
3. Carefully spoon the second different layer of beans onto the first in the jar.
4. Spoon layers of different kinds of beans on top of each other until you reach the top of the jar.
5. Screw the lid on tightly.

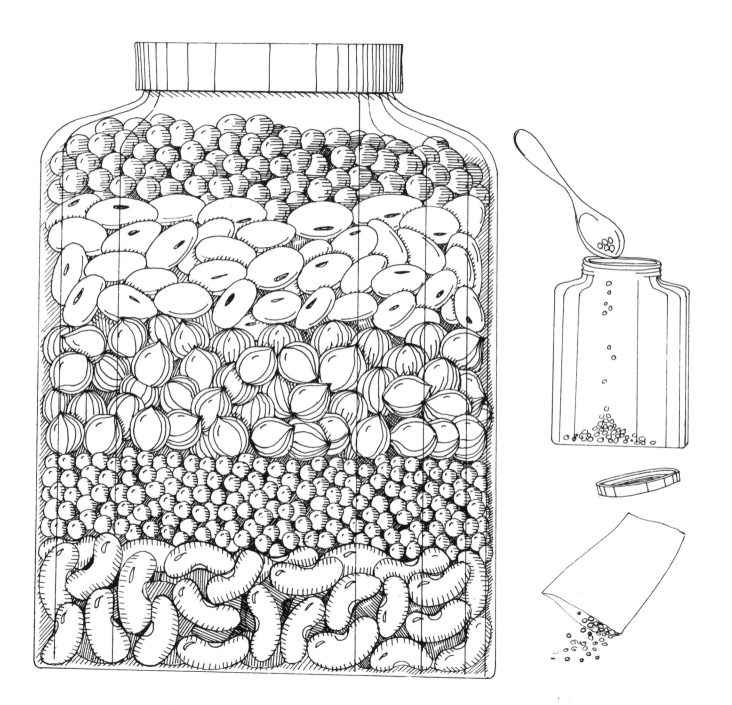

Hobnail Glasses

A hobnail is a short, thick-headed nail that was used at one time for shoeing horses. It is used today for attaching soles and heels to shoes and is a very strong nail to use. Hobnail glass got its name because it looks as if someone had driven hobnails into it. It's quite bumpy, but also very pretty at the same time. You can't make hobnail glass, but you can still see what it looks like. All it takes is some time and patience, some split peas, and a coating of white paint.

Things You Need

drinking glass or goblet
liquid white glue
paper cup or plate
paintbrush
dried split peas
white poster paint

Let's Begin

1. Wash the glass and dry it completely.
2. Pour a little white glue into a small paper cup or plate.
3. Decide on a design that you would like to create on the outside of the glass. It can be repetitive rows covering the entire glass, or just a simple design like a heart, see illustration.
4. Dip the end of a paintbrush handle into the liquid white glue. Dab the glue on the outside of the glass in the pattern you have decided upon.
5. Let the drops of glue dry just a few minutes, then put a split pea on each drop. Glue the flat side of the split pea to the glass.
6. Finish your design, and let the glued split peas dry overnight.
7. Paint the entire outside surface of the glass with white poster paint.
8. Use the glasses for holding a small bouquet of flowers.

Bean Bags

Probably one of the earliest games played by children was a toss game. A rock or some other object was used. Somewhere along the line a bean bag was invented. It is softer than a rock, and can be used in many different ways, such as a pincushion or a paperweight. The bean bag has always been used for games like hot potato (keep the bean bag in the air and not in your hands as you toss it around a circle of players). If you have never played with a bean bag, it's time you did. You and your friends can spend hours creating games and having fun with one another.

Things You Need

scissors
scrap felt
liquid white glue
lentils

Let's Begin

1. Cut two circles of the same size from scrap pieces of felt.
2. Decorate one or both circles with felt cut- outs in one of the designs shown in the illustrations: small circles and a smile make a Happy Face; two bars with shorter cross bars make a Baseball; a number 1 and a cent sign (¢) make a Penny; a circle with scallops makes a Flower. Or make up your own designs.
3. Squeeze liquid white glue along the edges of the design pieces. Glue the felt shapes onto the circles in their proper design.
4. Turn over the circle with the design facing down.
5. Squeeze liquid white glue around the edge of the circle with the design. Leave a little bit of the edge unglued for an opening.
6. Place the other circle over the glued circle.
7. Press the two circles together with your hands.
8. Let the circles dry overnight.
9. Spoon dried lentils into the opening of the glued circles. Fill half full.
10. Squeeze glue onto the open edges of the circles. Press together with your fingers.
11. When the newly glued edge of the circle has dried, use the bags in tossing and catching games.

Birdseed Squiggles

You can make a million-and-one different designs with Birdseed Squiggles. No two will ever be the same. You can use these crazy crafts to decorate your room. (Make sure your pet parakeet doesn't get hungry because you've taken all his seeds to make the squiggles!)

Things You Need

liquid white glue
waxed paper
birdseed
spoon
paper bag
string

Let's Begin

1. Remove the cap of a bottle of liquid white glue. Squeeze a squiggly design on a sheet of waxed paper, Fig. a. Be very careful when using the glue not to allow too much to come out of the bottle so that you get lumpy lines.
2. With a spoon, slowly sprinkle birdseed over the squiggly design, Fig. b. Be sure that the birdseed covers all of the glue.
3. Let the design dry overnight.
4. When dry, tilt the waxed paper into the paper bag to remove and save all of the extra seeds that did not dry on the glue.
5. Carefully peel away the waxed paper from the hardened seed squiggle.
6. Tie a length of string into a loop in the squiggle and knot it.
7. Hang the squiggle in a window or on a wall.

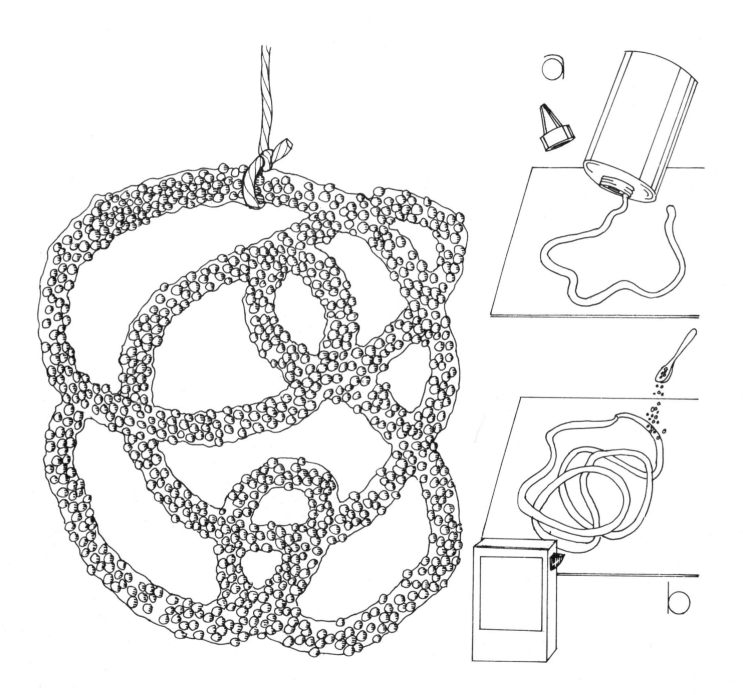

Seeded Pencil Holder Can

If you like to draw and write, you will need a place to keep your pencils and crayons. A tin can is an ideal pencil holder. It may not be pretty to look at with all of the writing on it, however. To make it more attractive, add a seeded cover to the outside of the can. You create the design in this interesting craft.

Things You Need

scissors
construction paper
coffee can
newspaper
liquid white glue
paper cup
paintbrush
melon, sunflower, bird, or spice seeds
tape

Let's Begin

1. Cut a piece of construction paper as tall as a coffee can and long enough to fit around the can with a little extra length.
2. Lay the construction paper on the newspaper.
3. Pour liquid white glue into a paper cup.
4. Paint a section of the construction paper with the glue, a little bit in from the end, Fig. a.
5. Sprinkle one kind of seed to the glued area.
6. Blow away any seeds that have not fallen onto the glue.
7. Paint another area with glue and sprinkle on another kind of seed.
8. Again, blow away any extra seeds.
9. Cover the paper with seeded areas. Do not add seeds to the ends of the paper. They will be taped together around the can.
10. Let the paper dry overnight.
11. Carefully roll the seeded paper around the can, Fig. b.
12. Overlap the ends that have no seeds glued to them. Tape or glue them together.
13. Brush glue on the part of the paper that has no seeds, Fig. c.
14. Sprinkle seeds on the glued surface.
15. When dry, paint these seeds with liquid white glue. Put pencils or whatever in the can.

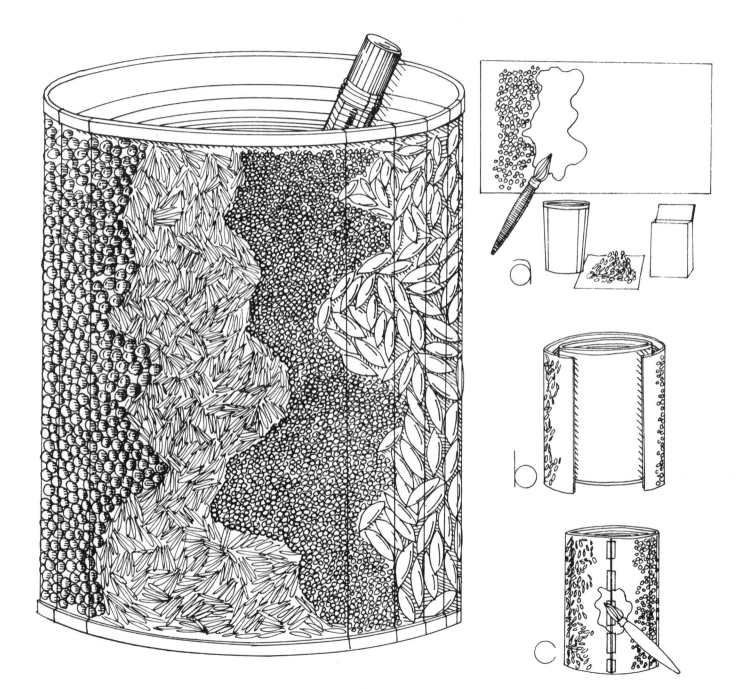

Melon Seed Necklace

Ever since people began to wear jewelry, natural things were strung and worn around the neck and wrists. Indians used shells for necklaces; some tribes in Africa use bones; and whale teeth and tusks are used by the Eskimos. Seeds were also used as beads. They were strung by themselves, or mixed with some of the items just mentioned. The necklace in this craft uses only seeds. Whatever melon your family enjoys, save and use the seeds from it. If your family enjoys all types of melon, you will have a large collection of neckware.

Things You Need

cantaloupe or honeydew melon seeds
box of dye or food coloring
small bowl
spoon
paper towel
needle and thread

Let's Begin

1. Wash the seeds.
2. Mix dye according to package directions in a small bowl, or use food coloring, and add the seeds.
3. Remove the seeds with a spoon from the coloring after a short time, and place them on a paper towel.
4. Let the seeds dry overnight.
**5. Thread a needle with sewing thread and knot the ends of the thread.
**6. Sew the seeds onto the thread, see illustration.
**7. Cut away the needle after you finish threading all of the seeds. Knot the ends of the thread together.

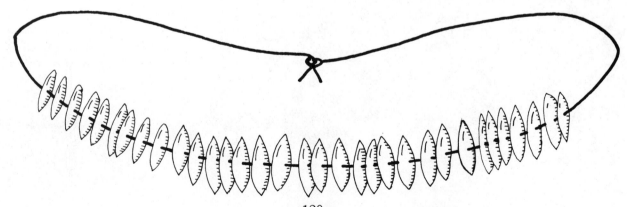

Which came first, the chicken or the egg?

Which came first, the chicken or the egg?

Do you know which came first? Wait a minute. Chickens come from eggs, so the egg must have come first. But eggs come from chickens... It's all rather confusing if you stop to think about it. Better not spend too much time trying to solve this mystery. Nobody has yet been able to pick one or the other for first place. Might as well just be happy that there are chickens laying eggs so that you can look at them, eat them, and—you guessed it—make things from them.

This chapter shows you many crafts you can make with eggs, or more exactly, egg shells. All of the projects require whole empty eggs, half egg shells, or pieces of egg shell. Eggs are fun to work with because of their shape and because they can be painted, dyed, and colored with crayons. Since they have an inside, you can put things in them and use them in all ways to make fun toys and pretty decorations for your room. If a member of the family is celebrating a birthday, many lovely gifts can be made with egg shells.

It would be nice if you could get some of the wonderfully colored eggs the wild birds lay. It *is* possible for you to locate such priceless egg shells. The next time you are in the woods, look on the ground under trees for blue, green, brown or speckled pieces of egg. But don't worry, really, if you can't find any. You will have more than your share of fun with the plain old chicken eggs to be found in your local supermarket.

Blown Eggs

There are many projects in this chapter that require blown eggs—eggs that have had their contents removed without breaking the shells. You have to use blown eggs in these crafts because the egg—and the craft—will go bad if you leave the white and yolk inside the shell. Blow out eggs whenever they are to be used for cooking and save the shells for future craftwork.

Things You Need

straight pin
egg, at room temperature
bowl or dish

Let's Begin

**1. Twist a pin into the top or pointed end of an egg. Twist back and forth until you break through the shell, Fig. a.

**2. Keep twisting the pin into the egg until you break through the membrane that lies just under the shell.

3. Remove the pin.

**4. Make another hole by twisting the pin into the other end of the egg just as you did before, Fig. b.

5. Make this hole a little larger by carefully poking away some of the shell with the tip of the pin, Fig. c.

6. Remove the pin.

7. Hold the egg over a bowl or dish, with the large hole down.

8. Blow through the small hole. The egg will flow slowly through the larger hole, Fig. d.

9. Rinse the egg under cold running water. Do not wash with soap.

10. Store blown egg in a used egg carton. Do not use until thoroughly dry.

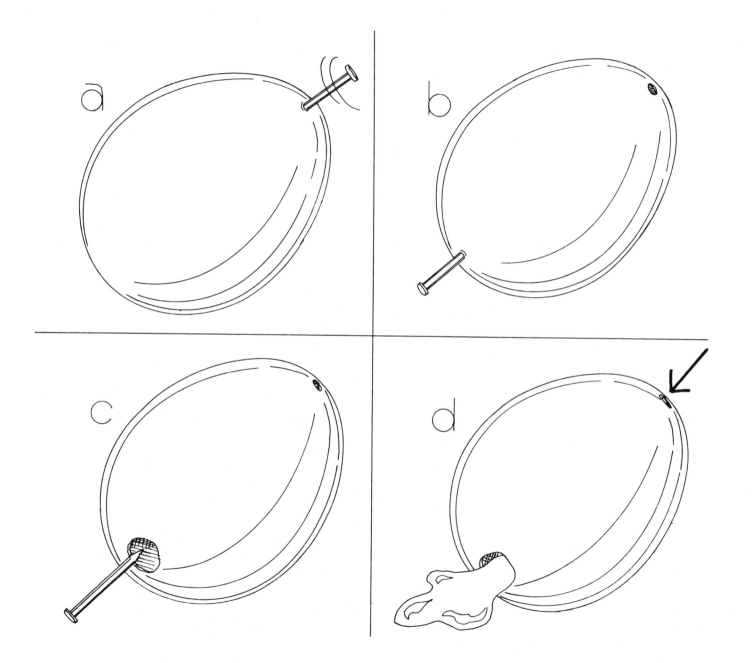

Batik Eggs

It's fun coloring eggs during the Easter season. One way to do this is to use dyes and a white crayon. This is a form of batik. Batik is a method of putting designs on fabric or a smooth surface by using dyes and wax. You put wax where you don't want any color—dyes can't penetrate it. Batiking is really very simple to do. With a little patience you will create a beautiful egg that any chicken would be proud to sit on.

Things You Need

blown (or hard-boiled) eggs, see page 124
white crayon
egg dye or food coloring
paper cups or glasses
spoon
paper towels
rubber cement

Let's Begin

CRAYON BATIK
1. Draw a free-hand squiggly design over a blown or hard-boiled egg with a white crayon, Fig. a.
2. Mix egg dye or food coloring in a paper cup or a glass that is three-quarters filled with water.
3. Dye the egg by dipping in the coloring solution. Because blown eggs are lighter than hard-boiled eggs, you may have to hold down a blown egg with a spoon.
4. Carefully lift the egg out of the dye with a spoon.
5. Place the egg on paper towels to dry.

RUBBER CEMENT EGGS
1. Dip the brush on the cap of a rubber cement bottle into the glue. Dribble squiggly designs onto a blown or hard-boiled eggs, Fig. b. Do not brush the rubber cement on the eggs as if you were gluing something.
2. Hold the egg a few minutes until the rubber cement dries.
3. Dye the egg just as you did for the Crayon Batik egg. Dry thoroughly.
4. Rub the rubber cement off the dried egg with your fingers.

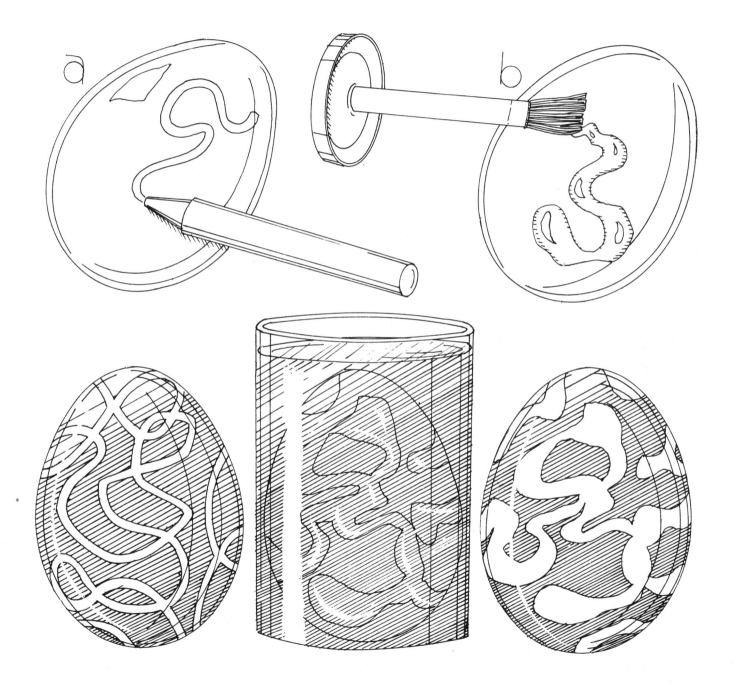

a

b

Patchwork Eggs

A craft your great-grandmother may have done was patchwork quilting. During olden times, women used every scrap of material they had saved and sewed them together. They used this patchwork sheet to make clothing, curtains, or bedspreads. You won't need a needle and thread for this patchwork project. A dab of glue and an egg will create an old-fashioned delight for you or as a gift.

Things You Need

scissors
colored tissue paper or scraps of fabric
liquid white glue
paper cup
paintbrush
blown (or hard-boiled) eggs, see page 124

Let's Begin

1. Cut colored tissue paper or scrap fabric into square or rectangular shapes. Each shape should be about the size of postage stamps.
2. Pour liquid white glue into a paper cup.
3. Paint an area of the egg with glue, Fig. a.
4. Place the first tissue or fabric cutout on the glued part of the egg, Fig. b.
5. Paint another section of the egg with glue.
6. Place the second tissue or fabric cutout overlapping the first on the egg. They can overlap as much as you like and in any direction, Fig. c.
7. Cover the entire surface of the egg in this manner with either tissue or fabric shapes. If some ends turn out not to be glued down on the egg, lift them up and add a bit of glue.
8. Smooth out all of the glued patches with your fingers before you set the egg aside to dry.

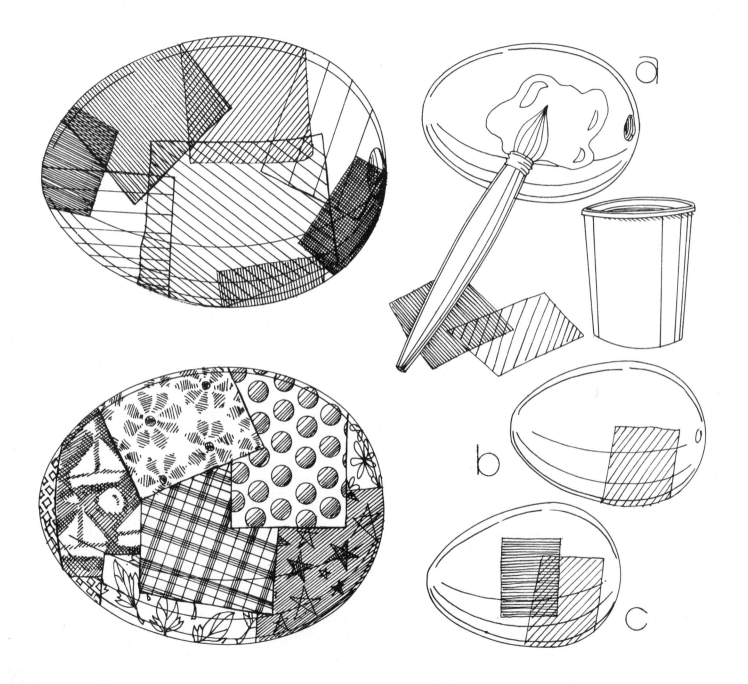

Egg Paperweights

If your homework papers get lost or fall under the table, then you need a paperweight to keep them in place. Mom or Dad may need one for their important papers. No matter who needs a paperweight, they are fun to make and decorate.

Things You Need

blown eggs, see page 124
straight pin
paper collar, see Egg Characters, page 132
spoon
plaster of paris
paper cup
waxed paper or small funnel
egg dyes or food coloring
liquid white glue
colored yarn or thick cord
scissors
sequins
gold or colored stick-on paper stars

Let's Begin

**1. Poke away at the larger hole of a blown egg with a straight pin until the hole is the size of a shirt button or could take the spout of a small funnel, Fig. a.

2. Make a paper collar for the egg to stand in. See Egg Characters, page 132, for directions.

3. Stand the egg in the collar with the large hole facing up.

4. Put several spoonfuls of plaster of paris in the papercup. Stirring all the while, add water until the mixture looks a little thicker than milk.

5. Place the spout of a real or paper funnel into the hole. To make a paper funnel, roll waxed paper into a cone and cut open the tip, Fig. b.

6. Pour or spoon the liquid plaster into the egg through the funnel, Fig. c. Remove the funnel, and fill the egg to the very top with the plaster of paris mixture.

7. Let the plaster that is in the egg dry overnight. If the plaster shrinks in the egg, add freshly mixed plaster the following day.

8. Dye the egg if you desire.

9. Squeeze liquid white glue onto the egg in rings or in a checkerboard pattern, Fig. d.

10. Place pieces of yarn on top of the glue lines.

11. Trim the ends of the yarn with scissors.

12. Use liquid white glue to decorate the eggs with sequins or stick-on paper stars.

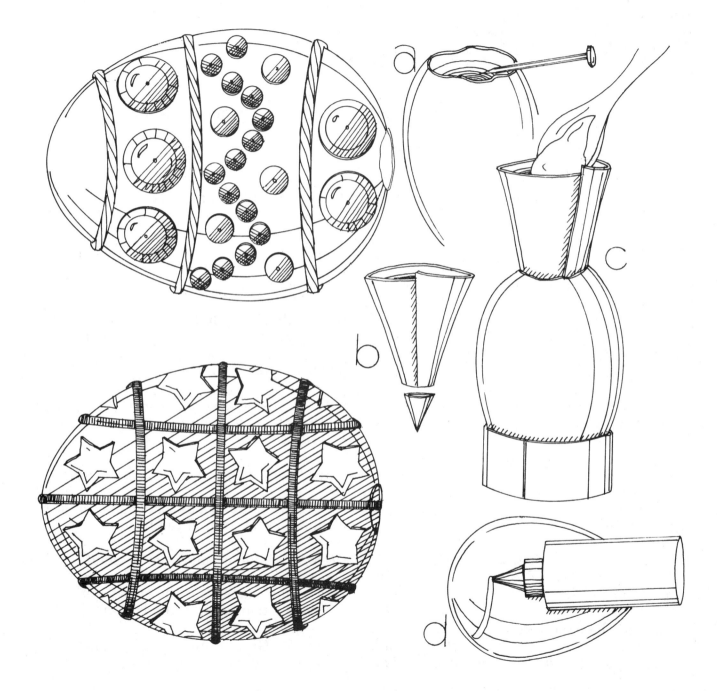

Egg Characters

Who are your favorite characters? You may have gone to the circus and loved the clown. What about that visitor from outer space you saw in a scary movie? Whoever or whatever they are, you can have your favorite characters with you whenever you want. All it takes is a carton full of blown eggs and a little imagination.

Things You Need

blown (or hard-boiled) eggs, see page 124
crayons
egg dye or food coloring
paper cups
spoon
paper towels
scissors
colored construction paper
liquid white glue
feather
yarn
beads or beans
pipe cleaner

Let's Begin

1. Draw a face on a blown egg with crayons.
2. Mix egg dye or food coloring as for Batik Eggs, page 126, and dye the eggs.
3. Make paper collars, which will act as little stands to hold the eggs upright. To do so, cut a strip from colored construction paper, Fig. a. Roll the strip into a circle overlapping the ends until you have a collar that eggs will rest in snugly, Figs. b and c. Cut any excess off the strip ends. Using this strip as a guide, make as many collars as you will need. Draw designs on strips with crayons and glue the ends together.
4. Finish by decorating the eggs to make the characters below.

RABBIT: Glue pointed colored construction paper ears to the head.

LADY: Make a hat from a circle of colored construction paper with a smaller circle cut out of the middle of it, see illustration. Add a paper feather.

INDIAN: Glue colored construction paper feathers to a paper circle headband made like the egg collar.

MAN: Glue tied-yarn hair to the head.

MARTIAN: Glue beads or beans to a pipe cleaner. Twist around the head.

CLOWN: Make a hat from a small colored construction paper cone (roll a square of paper into a cone shape, tape the ends together) and add paper trimming to the bottom edge.

MONKEY: Glue round colored construction paper ears to egg, see illustration.

a

b

c

Egg Village

Now you can be the builder of your own village. All it takes is a half-a-dozen blown eggs, and you'll be just about ready to set up shop. You will need a few improvements, perhaps, before the permanent residents move into their new community.

Things You Need

6 blown eggs, see page 124
crayons
egg dye or food coloring
paper cups
spoon
paper towels
scissors
heavy cardboard
liquid white glue
colored construction paper
Easter grass (artificial toy grass, purchasable at the five-and-ten-cent store)
waxed paper
paintbrush
twigs
play clay (any non-hardening clay)
candy wafers and spearmint leaves

Let's Begin

1. Draw windows and doors on blown eggs with crayons, Fig. a. Mix egg dye or food coloring as you did for Batik Eggs, page 126, and dye the eggs.
2. Cut a square of heavy cardboard as large as you want the area of your village to be.
3. Squeeze big dabs of liquid white glue onto the heavy cardboard where you want the egg houses to go. Wait five minutes and then place the decorated eggs on the glue. Allow the glue to dry completely.
4. Fold rectangular pieces of colored construction paper in half for the roofs. Trim the folded paper to fit the eggs.
5. Draw a roof design on the roofs with a crayon, Fig. b.
6. Glue the roofs to the eggs with the liquid white glue.
7. Cut some Easter grass into little pieces like confetti and place on waxed paper.
8. Pour some liquid white glue in a paper cup.
9. Paint the tips of the twigs with glue.
10. Roll the glued twigs in the cut-up grass.
11. Stick balls of play clay to the cardboard near the eggs, and stand the twig trees in the clay.
12. Squeeze squiggles of glue over the cardboard.
13. Scatter Easter grass over the squiggles on the cardboard.
14. Add a candy wafer path and spearmint leaf bushes, see illustration.

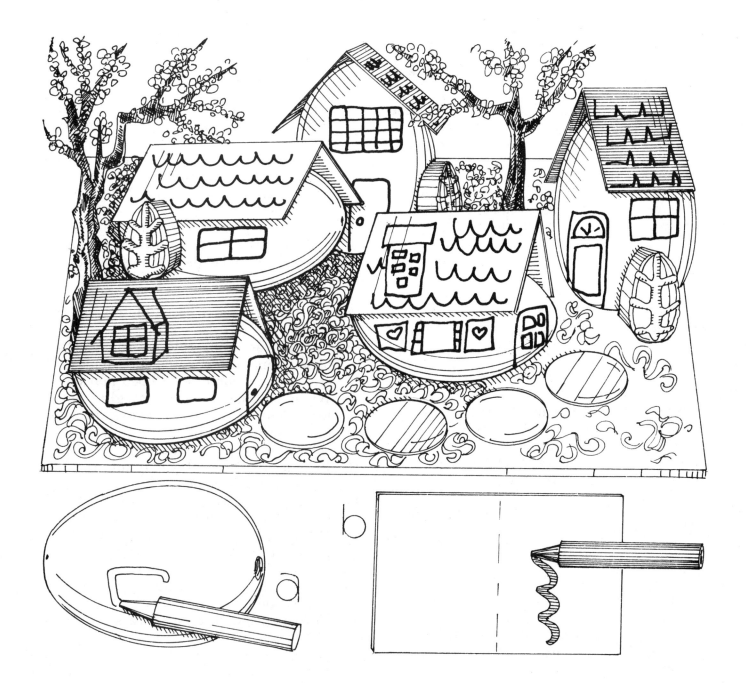

Pot of Tulips

You don't want to tiptoe through these tulips. They break too easily. As a matter of fact, they are as fragile as a carton of fresh farm eggs (they *are* eggs!). Save the cracked egg shell halves that are usually thrown away when eggs are cooked, wash carefully, and let dry. Now you can use these egg shell halves to make a pretty pot of flowers for the kitchen or your bedroom.

Things You Need

cracked egg shell halves
egg dye or food coloring
paper cups
spoon
paper towels
scissors
paper or plastic drinking straws
liquid white glue
colored construction paper
colored felt-tipped markers or crayons
play clay (any non-hardening clay)
small flower pot
Easter grass (artificial grass, purchasable at
   the five-and-ten-cent store)

Let's Begin

1. Choose the best-shaped egg shell halves you have saved.
2. Mix egg dye or food coloring as you did for Batik Eggs, page 126, and dye the egg shells.
**3. Stems will be made from straws. Cut slits into one end of each of the straws with scissors, Fig. a.
4. Push back the two cut ends of each straw. Flatten out the curve of the ends with your fingers, Fig. b. Paper straws work best.
5. Squeeze liquid white glue on the cut ends. Let the glue dry several minutes.
6. Press the glued ends of each straw to the bottom ends of dyed egg shell halves, Fig. c.
7. Let the straws dry completely on the shells.
8. Cut leaves from colored construction papers and draw veins on them with crayons or colored felt-tipped markers.
9. When the straws are dry, glue paper leaves onto them. Paper straws and some plastic straws can be colored green with a colored felt-tipped marker.
10. Push a big ball of play clay into the bottom of the flower pot.
11. Push the straws into the clay.
12. Cut a strip of colored construction paper. Cut slits into the paper. Don't cut completely through the paper, Fig. d.
13. Roll the fringed paper and glue, Fig. e.
14. Glue these tassels inside each tulip, see illustration.
15. Fill the pot with Easter grass.

a

b

c

d

e

Egg Shell Mosaic

Looking through a kaleidoscope is like seeing a continuous, always-changing mosaic. Mosaics are paintings made of bits of glass or tile. Glass and tile aren't the only things that you can use to make mosaics. The butterfly mosaic you are going to make is made with egg shells that have been broken into small pieces. Once all of the pieces have been dyed, a butterfly as real as life will bring springtime to your special room.

Things You Need

pencil
heavy paper or cardboard
liquid white glue
cord or colored yarn
scissors
egg dye or food coloring
paper cups
paper towels
spoon
cracked egg shells
waxed paper
rolling pin
paintbrush

Let's Begin

1. Draw a simple butterfly design for your mosaic on a piece of cardboard or heavy paper with a pencil, Fig. a.
2. Squeeze a line of liquid white glue on all the pencil lines of the drawing, Fib. b.
3. Lay cord or yarn along the glued lines, Fig. c. Cut away the extra yarn or cord with scissors.
4. Mix egg dye or food coloring as you did for Batik Eggs, page 126, and dye cracked egg shells.
5. Place the dyed egg shells between two sheets of waxed paper.
6. Crush the shells by rolling a rolling pin over the waxed paper.
7. Pour liquid white glue into a paper cup.
8. Brush an enclosed area of the design with a thick coating of liquid white glue, Fig. d.
9. Sprinkle the crushed egg shells onto the glued area, Fig. e.
10. Repeat gluing and sprinkling shells, filling in all areas of your design.
11. Let the shells dry overnight.
12. When the designs are dry, tip the paper to remove any shells that did not stick to the glue. Brush a coating of glue thinned with a little water over the entire surface of the shell design.

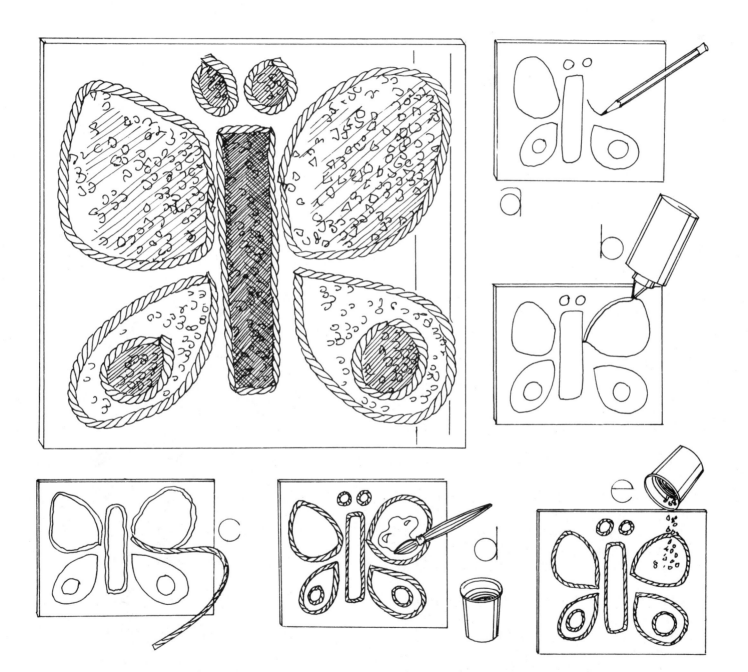

Egg Tree

Have you ever seen a tree with eggs hanging from it? The only way you will ever see one is to make one. You will need a small branch and some decorated blown eggs to complete this unusual tree.

Things You Need

small tin can
plaster of paris
paper cup
small branch
scissors
ribbon
liquid white glue
blown decorated eggs, given in this chapter

Let's Begin

1. Remove the label from the tin can by soaking it in warm water. Dry completely.
2. Put several spoonfuls of plaster of paris into a paper cup. Stirring all the while, add water until the mixture looks like heavy cream.
3. Pour the plaster of paris mixture into the tin can almost to the top.
4. Wait a few minutes and then stand the branch straight in the plaster.
5. Cut the ribbon into small pieces. Tie a knot in the center of each piece. Glue ribbon at the knots to the tops of the eggs.
6. When the glue is dry, tie the eggs to different limbs of the branch.
7. Tie a ribbon bow around the can.

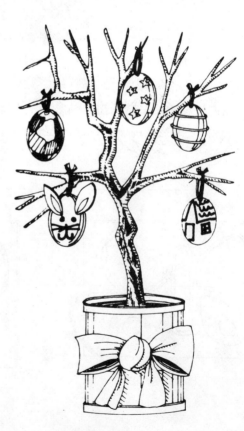

Stones
can be found
everywhere

Stones can be found everywhere

Stones are among the most common objects found almost everywhere. By the sea, up a mountain, even in the city, you will see stones of all sizes, shapes, and colors. Some are opaque, and some you can see through. Stones, or rocks as we may sometimes call them, were formed in two ways. Some came from inside the center of the earth where it was very hot. Others were made by pressure for millions and millions of years. You might have a rock collection of your own own. If you do, you know how much fun it is collecting them.

Stones are used frequently in jewelry when they are of special value. Pendants, bracelets, and rings are made with stones of many kinds. Besides starting a stone collection, there are lots of other things you can do with them. As you read through this chapter, you will see how you can make stone people and animals, as well as games and stone sculptures. Even if you never liked stones before, after finishing some of the crafts, you may be hooked on a new hobby.

Now is the time to start collecting stones in all sizes, shapes, and colors, and to store them away for future projects. (Besides making crafts, stones can be used in fish tanks, in flower pots, or when playing with your favorite toys.) Make sure that you don't throw stones at anyone or at anything, though—they can hurt. Better use them to make one of the beautiful creations that follow.

Rock Collection

Do you collect rocks or stones? If you do, and they are here and there in your dresser drawers or a toy chest, why not display them neatly? Save as many egg cartons as you can for this project. They make good collection boxes because you can put one stone in each of the egg compartments. If you don't have a collection of pretty stones, start getting one together. Wherever you go with your friends or family, look around for interesting stones. Stone collecting can become a facinating hobby for you. There are many books that will help you identify all of the rocks you collect. Why not start collecting now?

Things You Need

scissors
colored construction paper
egg carton
liquid white glue
12 very special stones
colored felt-tipped markers or crayons

Let's Begin

1. Cut a piece of colored construction paper large enough to cover entirely the outside lid of an egg carton.
2. Using liquid white glue, glue the cut paper to the top of the lid. Make sure all of the edges are glued down neatly.
3. Wash and dry your special stones.
4. Glue one stone into each compartment of the egg carton.
5. Use a crayon or colored felt-tipped marker to write where the rocks were collected, and the type of rocks they are, on the carton.

Indian Pebble Game

The Indians used natural things in their games. They played many games that involved rolling stones. Signs and symbols were painted or carved on the stones, and games of skill and luck were played with them. This game is fun to play anywhere, especially when the rain is pelting against your window. This is the time to gather all of the braves together for a day of skill and excitement.

Things You Need

15 smooth pebbles (small stones)
nailpolish
scissors
colored construction paper
coffee can
colored felt-tipped markers or crayons
tape

Let's Begin

1. Wash and dry the pebbles.
2. Paint an X on five of the stones with nailpolish.
3. Paint an O on five of the stones with nailpolish.
4. Paint a Z on five of the stones with nailpolish.
5. Let the nailpolish on all the stones dry.
6. Cut a piece of colored construction paper as high as the coffee can and long enough to wrap around it.
7. Draw Indian designs on the paper with crayons or colored felt-tipped markers, see illustration for some examples.
8. Wrap the paper around the can, and tape the paper ends together.
9. When the painted letters on the pebbles are dry, place them in the can.
10. To play the game, each player in turn puts his hand in the can and pulls out one pebble. When all of the pebbles are picked from the can, the one who has the most of one kind of letter wins the round. Repeat several times.

Basket of Fruit

Fruit arranged in a pretty way in a basket looks good enough to be eaten—and usually is. The stone fruit we will make in this craft would be hard to swallow, but makes a beautiful decoration nonetheless. It will be a lovely addition to any room in your home.

Things You Need

different sized stones (round and smooth)
poster paints
paintbrushes
liquid white glue
green construction paper
scissors
pipe cleaners

Let's Begin

1. Choose stones of appropriate shapes, as indicated below, and decorate to make fruit.

APPLE (A). Paint a medium-sized stone red with a pink highlight. Glue on a green construction paper leaf.

ORANGE (B). Paint a medium-sized stone orange with brown speckles, and add a brown star on top.

MELON (C). Paint a large stone green with light green squiggles going from one end of the stone to the other.

PLUM (D). Paint a small stone purple with a pink circle highlight.

STRAWBERRY (E). Paint a tiny stone red with black speckles. Glue on a green construction paper star-leaf.

PEACH (F). Paint a medium-sized stone pink with a yellow circle highlight. Glue on a green construction paper leaf.

BLACKBERRY (G). Paint tiny stones black with blue dots.

GRAPEFRUIT (H). Paint a medium-large stone yellow with brown speckles and add a brown star on top.

LEMON OR LIME (I). Paint a small oblong stone yellow or green with brown speckles and add a star on top.

PEAR (J). Paint a medium-sized oblong stone yellow or light-green with a white circle highlight. Glue on a green paper leaf.

GRAPES (K). Glue small stones together with liquid white glue. When dry, paint them purple or light-green. Glue on a large green construction paper leaf. Glue two twisted pipe cleaners to the cluster for vines.

People and Pets

Creatures made of stone? It sounds like they might come from outer space. Not really. They come from your neighborhood—at least the stones you make them from do. Look carefully for the stones of the right size, and this happy family of stone creatures can be all yours. With paint and dabs of glue, their stone faces will come to life.

Things You Need

large, medium, and small flattish stones
waxed paper
liquid white glue
poster paints
paintbrushes
ice-cream stick

Let's Begin

BOY
1. Place two small flat stones on a sheet of waxed paper. These will be the boy's feet.
2. Squeeze a large dab of liquid white glue on the top of the stones.
3. Let the glue dry for five minutes, and place a medium-sized stone body on top of the feet.
4. Let all the stones dry.
5. When dry, squeeze a dab of glue on top of the body, wait five minutes, and add a smaller stone for the head.
6. When the stones have dried, paint the fig-ure to resemble a boy, using poster paints, see illustration.

MOTHER
1. Place a large stone on a sheet of waxed paper.
2. Using liquid white glue, glue two medium-sized stones on top of each other, and then glue both onto the top of the large stone, see illustration.
3. Glue a small stone for the hair bun onto the very top of the figure.
4. Let all the stones dry.
5. Break an ice-cream stick in half, and glue the halves onto the figure for the arms.
6. Using poster paints, paint the figure to resemble a mother, see illustration.

DOG
1. Place four small flat stones on a sheet of waxed paper. These will be the dog's feet.
2. Using liquid white glue, glue a medium-sized stone body to the four feet.
3. Glue a small stone head onto one side of the body stone, see illustration.
4. Glue another small stone onto the other side of the body stone for a tail.
5. Glue tiny pebbles to the head for the ears, see illustration.
6. Let all the stones dry.
7. Paint the figure to resemble a dog, see il-lustration.

Stone Sculptures

Have you ever poured wet sand on top of itself to make strange, icicle-like forms? If you have, then you know what interesting sculptures you can create. Stone sculptures look almost like sand sculptures. They are wide at the bottom and thin at the top. Create a dozen or so of these sculpture groups and make an outer space scene, or just place individual sculpture groups anywhere you like about your room.

Things You Need

disposable aluminum pie tin
flat, smooth beach pebbles (small stones) of different sizes
liquid white glue

Let's Begin

1. Turn the pie tin upside down. Make indentations in the bottom of the tin with the largest stones wherever you want to build a sculpture.

2. Squeeze liquid white glue into the indentations in the pie tin.
3. Place the largest pebbles onto the glued indentations.
4. Let the pebbles dry completely. Then squeeze a dab of glue onto the top of each pebble and allow to dry for about five minutes before carefully adding a layer of smaller pebbles. Let the new layer of pebbles dry completely.
5. Squeeze a dab of glue onto the top of the new layer of pebbles and let dry for five minutes before adding more pebbles. Be sure each layer of pebbles is completely dry before adding more glue and pebble layers. You will be building sculptures from large to increasingly smaller pebbles.
6. When this set of glued pebbles has dried, add another set just as you did with the last.
7. Continue building sculptures in this way. Make some sculptures taller than others. Be sure to let the glue dry for five minutes on one layer before adding another.

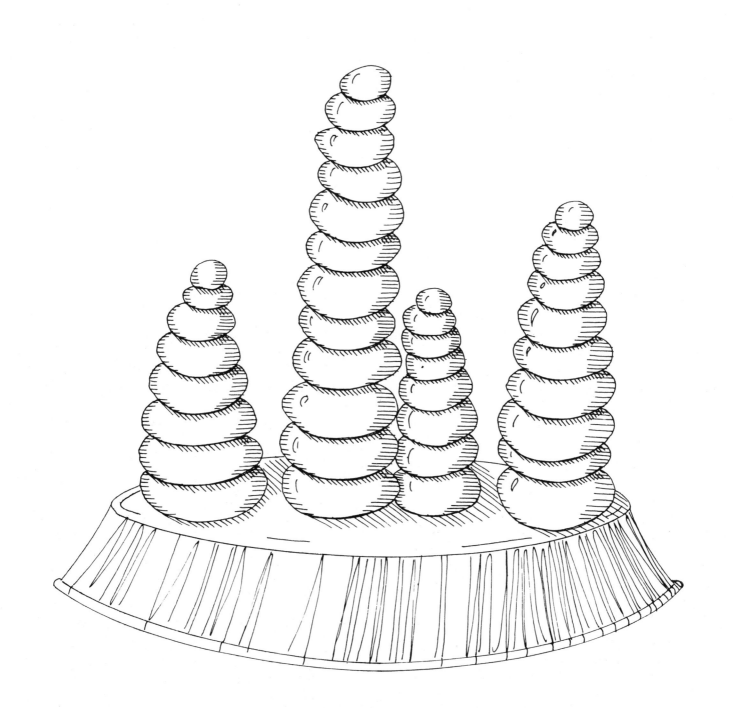

Rock Pendant

Rocks can be found in many different colors. This project asks that you look for the most beautiful rock you can find. Don't just choose any stone. Look for one that is shiny, colorful, or in some way interesting or unusual. If you have a back yard, there is probably a wonderful rock just waiting to be wrapped with yarn and worn as a pendant around your neck.

Things You Need

beautiful rock
colored yarn
scissors
liquid white glue
paper cup
waxed paper
paintbrush

Let's Begin

1. Wash and dry your rock.
2. Place the rock in the center of a length of yarn and wrap the rock by twisting the two ends of yarn in every direction around it, Fig. a.
3. Tie the two ends of the yarn tightly at the top of the rock with a double knot, Fig. a.
4. Make a loop in the yarn by tying the two ends of the yarn into a second double knot a little up from the first knot, Fig. b.
5. Trim the ends of the yarn with scissors.
6. Pour a little liquid white glue into a paper cup.
7. Place the wrapped rock on a sheet of waxed paper.
8. Paint the entire rock and yarn with a thin coating of liquid white glue, Fig. c. Use your paintbrush for this. Be sure the loop at the top remains open.
9. Let the glue dry.
10. When dry, slip a piece of yarn through the yarn loop.
11. Knot the two ends of the yarn to make a necklace that will fit over your head.

a

b

c

Mosaic in Plaster

The use of stones to create pretty mosaic designs is not a new art form. Stones were used to make mosaic floors many thousands of years ago. They were set in cement, and beautiful designs were created. Many ancient palaces have mosaic floors, walls, and ceilings, and all were done in bits of cut stone. Your mosaic will add an old-world tradition to your new-world bedroom.

Things You Need

bottom of a small gift box
sheet of aluminum foil
cord
coffee can
plaster of paris
long stirring stick
food coloring
plastic spoon
small smooth stones
scissors

Let's Begin

1. Line the inside of the bottom half of a gift box with a sheet of aluminum foil. Be sure to press the foil into the corners.
2. If you plan to hang your mosaic, punch two holes on the underside of the box near the top. Insert a piece of cord, and tie the ends loosely inside the box, Fig. a.
3. Fill the coffee can about half-full with plaster of paris.
4. Stirring all the while, add water until the mixture looks like heavy cream. Add a little bit of food coloring if you wish the background of the mosaic to be colored.
5. Pour the plaster into the foil-lined box bottom, Fig. b.
6. Quickly spread and smooth the plaster evenly in the box bottom with the plastic spoon.
7. Push pebbles halfway into the plaster, creating a design, Fig. c. Work fast, because the plaster will dry quickly.
8. The plaster will be completely dry in an hour.
9. If you wish to take the mosaic out of the box, trim away any extra foil with scissors.

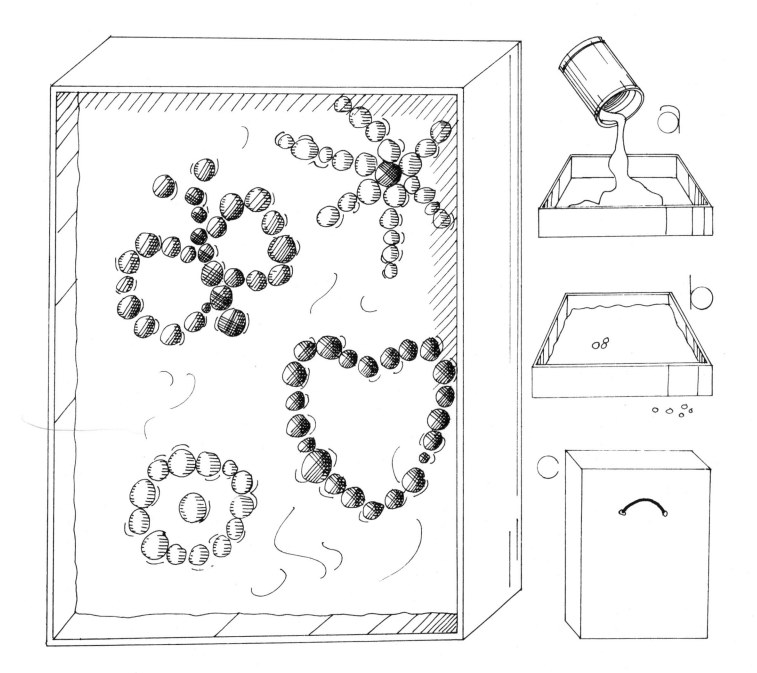

a

b
08

c

Stone Paperweights

Stones are very heavy and so can make excellent paperweights. For this project, look for stones with interesting shapes and fascinating colors. (You might even find many-colored stones or ones with stripes going all around them.) Paperweights make wonderful presents for any member of your family.

Things You Need

large smooth stones
poster paints
paintbrush
waxed paper
liquid white glue
paper cup

Let's Begin

1. Wash and dry a large smooth stone.
2. Using poster paint, paint the entire stone a color of your choice. If the stone is particularly beautiful in itself, you may wish to omit this step and skip to step 4.
3. Let the paint dry.
4. Paint a design on the stone that you like, or for the snail, paint a spiral line, see illustration for examples. Let the design dry.
5. Place the stone on a piece of waxed paper.
6. Pour liquid white glue into a paper cup, and carefully brush a coating of glue on the stone. Don't scrub on the glue or you may smudge your design.
7. Let the glue dry on the stone.
8. To make the snail's head, cut out a long-rounded shape and glue it to the bottom of the stone. Draw eyes on it.

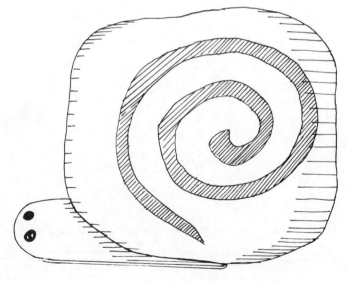

A shell
was once a home

A shell
was once a home

A sea shell that you collect at the shore was once a home, the living protective part of the soft creature within it. The shell grows with its "occupant." When that occupant dies, the shell does too (its the creature's outside skeleton, and like a human skeleton, it remains after the body is gone). The sea washes the empty shell to the shore. There you pick it up and probably wonder about what kind of strange and beautiful thing it is.

There are basically two shell types: the clam and the snail. If you are a practiced shell collector, you know that many varieties of these shells exist. The clam types are usually flat or dish-like, while the snail types are usually spiral or cone-shaped. Shellfish provide food for people and other animals, like seagulls. They even provide protective homes for some of the other creatures of the deep. The hermit crab will make an empty shell—a shell whose original occupant has died—his own home, while small fish will protect themselves under a clam shell to escape the hungry jaws of a larger fish. All shell inhabitants are among the earth's oldest living things.

It's wonderful to think about these things—to collect and look at sea shells—but did you know that shells can be used in wonderful craft projects? They can be used to decorate a comb, strung for a necklace, transformed into animals, and made into many more beautiful items. All it takes is some glue, string, paint, and a box of different type of shells. If you don't live near the ocean, don't worry. Hobby stores and other craft counters carry shells of all sizes and shapes. Mom and Dad will help you to locate the places where shells can be bought. It doesn't matter where you get your shells, really. As long as you have a few, a world of fun things to make is at your fingertips.

Shell Necklace and Pin

Shells can be used in many decorative crafts, but most craftsmen use these underwater treasures for jewelry. If you can get to the beach, collect a wide assortment of small shells. You can usually find them where the waves break on the shore. If you don't make it to the ocean, your local hobby store most probably carries bags of small, colored shells. Create an entire jewelry wardrobe with shells, a different design for every day of the week.

Things You Need

scissors
colored yarn or cord
liquid white glue
small shells
cardboard
heavy paper or fabric
safety pin
poster paints
paintbrush

Let's Begin

NECKLACE
1. Cut yarn into small pieces.
2. Tie a knot in the middle of each piece of yarn, Figs. a and b.
3. Squeeze a dab of liquid white glue into the opening or near the top of each sea shell.
4. Press the knots of the yarn pieces into the glue, Fig. c.
5. Let the yarn in the shells dry.
6. When dry, tie the shells onto a length of yarn at different intervals. The yarn should be long enough to make a necklace that will slip easily over your head when knotted.

PIN
1. Cut a round or oblong shape from the cardboard.
2. Cut a small paper or fabric hinge about the width of the closed safety pin and not much longer, Fig. d.
3. Slip the paper or fabric cutout through the closed safety pin, Fig. d. This will be the clasp.
4. Glue the back of the paper or fabric with the safety pin to the back of the cardboard near the top. Make sure you glue the part of the safety pin that doesn't open to the cardboard, not the other way around.
5. Paint the top side of the cardboard with poster paints.
6. Glue small sea shells in a pretty design to the painted side of the cardboard.

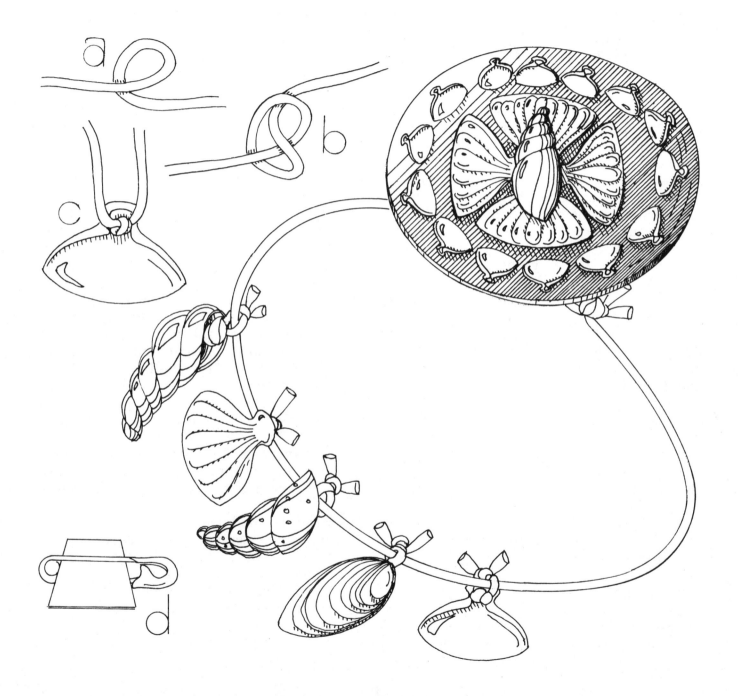

Slowpoke Turtle

It was the slowpoke turtle that managed to beat the speedy hare in that famous race you've undoubtedly heard about. Turtles can't move very fast, but when they have to go somewhere, usually nothing stops them. On your next trip to the beach, look for the makings of this slow-moving animal. You will need a large round shell, five small flat shells, and an oval-shaped shell. The best oval-shaped shell to use is a cowry shell, and you can purchase it at your local hobby or shell store if you can't find one. All of the shells you need can be bought in hobby stores.

Things You Need

liquid white glue
large, round shell
white drawing paper
scissors
four small flat shells
waxed paper
piece of broken shell
pipe cleaner
long, oval shell (cowry shell)
colored felt-tipped markers or crayons
paintbrush

Let's Begin

1. Squeeze liquid white glue around the bottom edge of the large, round shell, Fig a.

2. Place the glued side of the shell onto a piece of paper.
3. When the glue has dried, trim away the excess paper with scissors, Fig. b.
4. Squirt glue on the top of the four small flat shells.
5. Using the large, round shell as a guide, arrange the four shells on a sheet of waxed paper in "feet position," two on one side of the large, round shell, and two on the other side, Fig. c.
6. Place the large, round shell paper-side down over the four glued small shells.
7. Use the piece of broken shell for a tail. Put a dab of glue on top of it, and glue it under one end of the large shell.
8. Let the turtle dry.
9. Cut a pipe cleaner in half, and glue one of the pieces to the inside of the long, oval shell, Fig. d. Let it dry.
10. Gently push the other end of the pipe cleaner neck into the paper on the underside opposite the tail of the large, round shell.
11. Bend the shell head up, pushing all of the extra pipe cleaner into the paper, Fig. e.
12. Once the turtle's head is in place, glue the pipe cleaner to the paper.
13. When dry, draw eyes on the turtle's head using colored felt-tipped markers or crayons.

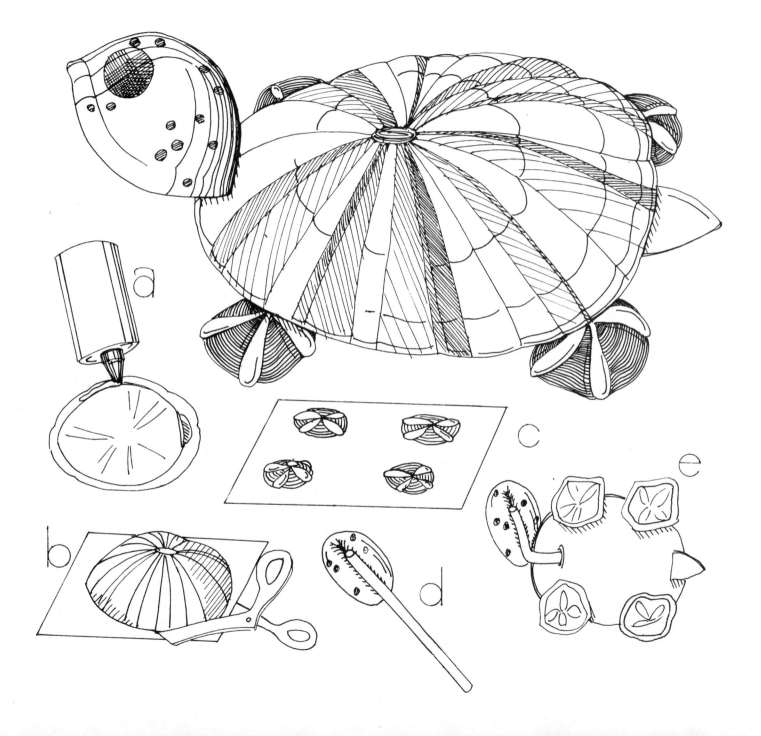

Butterfly Mobile

Butterflies appear to dance from one flower to another. This ballet is one of the main attractions of spring. If you enjoy watching a field of graceful butterflies, then a mobile of shell butterflies is what you need in your room.

Things You Need

pencil
tracing paper
scissors
cardboard
liquid white glue
flat shells of 2 different sizes or kinds (preferably mussel and scallop shells)
poster paints
paintbrush
pipe cleaners or drinking straws
beads
paper punch
yarn
plastic coffee can lid
paper clips

Let's Begin

1. Trace the butterfly body shape onto a sheet of tracing paper with a pencil.
2. Cut out the tracing.
3. Using the tracing as a pattern, trace the body shape onto a piece of cardboard.
4. Cut out the butterfly body from the cardboard.
5. Using liquid white glue, glue the bottom end of two large shells (mussel shells) to the top of the body shape at places marked by an X on the body shape in the book.
6. Glue two smaller shells (scallop shells) to the bottom of the body shape at places marked by an O on the body shape in the book.
7. Using poster paint, paint spots on the shells and eyes on the body.
8. Fold a pipe cleaner in half.
9. Glue a bead to each end of the pipe cleaner.
10. When the beads have dried, glue the folded point of the pipe cleaner to the back of the top of the butterfly body shape.
11. When the pipe cleaner has dried, punch a hole near the top of the butterfly's head with a paper punch.
12. Tie a piece of yarn through the hole, leaving one end long.
13. Make several more butterflies.
14. Punch well-spaced holes in the plastic coffee can lid with a paper punch, one hole for each butterfly you have made.
15. Push the yarn ends of each butterfly up through the holes in the lid.
16. Tie the ends of yarn to paper clips.
17. Punch two more holes opposite one another, near the edge of the lid.
18. Push two lengths of yarn down through the holes, and knot in place. Use these strands to hang your mobile.

Shell Flowers

On your next excursion to the seashore, gather a bagful of sea shells and save them for a pretty bouquet of shell flowers. Once you have made a lovely vase full of these "blossoms," your family and friends will enjoy looking at them just as they would the real thing.

Things You Need

small, flat shells (shells which look like flower petals)
liquid white glue
pipe cleaners

Let's Begin

1. Squeeze a large dab of liquid white glue onto the inside of the shells at their narrowest points.
2. Place one end of a pipe cleaner into the glue to form shell petals, Fig. a.
3. Let the glue dry completely.
4. Twist as many shell petals together as you want to form a flower, Fig. b. If you are lucky enough to have a long, cone-shaped shell, glue it onto a pipe cleaner and use it as a center petal for your flower.
5. Add a shell to the stem of a finished flower for a leaf, see illustration.
6. Make as many shell flowers as you like, and arrange them in an attractive vase or jar.

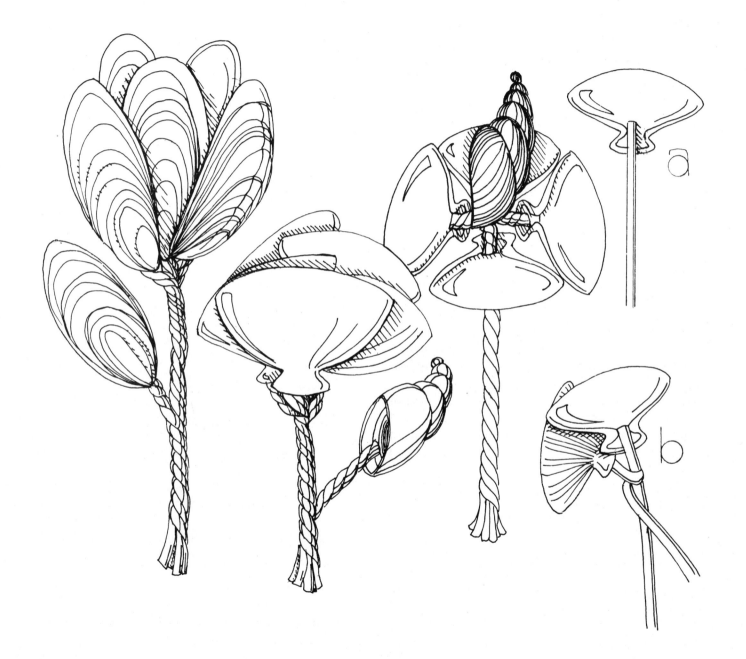

a

b

Picture Frame

Most picture frames you see in the stores are made of wood or metal. They are usually painted a solid color, or left unpainted. If you have pretty pictures you want framed and you don't want a plain-looking frame, use shells and cardboard to make as many frames as you need. Any picture will look great behind a shell-studded frame. All you need is a dab of glue, some paint, shells, and a piece of cardboard. You might want to surprise Mom and Dad with a beautifully framed picture of their favorite person, You.

Things You Need

scissors
heavy cardboard
pencil
ruler
poster paints
paintbrush
liquid white glue
different kinds of shells
tape

Let's Begin

1. Cut the cardboard to the size and shape you want your frame to be.
2. Draw a square or a rectangle in the center of the cardboard with a pencil and a ruler. There should be an equal border on all sides of the shape you draw.
**3. Cut out the inside shape with scissors.
4. Paint the frame with poster paint, and let it dry.
5. Using liquid white glue, glue shells on the dried cardboard frame in a pretty design.
6. Center your picture in the cutout area on the underside of the shell frame.
7. Tape the picture to the frame when it is in the right position.

Standing Planter

If you or any member of your family enjoys growing plants, then this craft is sure to please. To make it, you will need large sea clam shells. These are the ones people generally use for ashtrays or candy dishes. The sea clam shells are best found at the beach. Make many planters with them, and start yourself on a new hobby, growing flowers in your home. When your plants get too big for the shell, get a larger flower pot, or plant them in the garden. You may be the only horticulturist (a person who grows plants) on your block!

Things You Need
large sea clam shell
liquid white glue
three large beads or marbles
soil
seeds

Let's Begin

1. Turn the clam shell upside down.
2. Squeeze three large dabs of liquid white glue onto the shell as shown in the illustration.
3. Let the glue dry for five minutes on the shell.
4. Push the beads or marbles into the glue.
5. Let the glue dry overnight.
6. Turn the shell onto its bead legs.
7. Fill the shell with soil.
8. Plant a few seeds in the soil following all of the instructions given on the back of the seed package.
9. Water the seeds as the soil in the shell dries.

Collage Box

By now, you have probably collected quite a few seaside things for your craftwork. Why not display your salty treasures in a collage box? Collage boxes are very popular today. To make one, you begin by dividing a large box into smaller compartments. In each compartment you place one or more objects arranged in a pretty design. Shells are not the only things you can gather at the beach and use for your collage box. Pieces of coral, driftwood, sea glass, and shiny stones are other collectables that can be found near the surf. Collect a bagful of nature's wonders the next time you go to the beach (or, for that matter, anywhere you can). You may want more than one collage box for all of the treasures you bring home.

Things You Need

paintbrush
poster paints
bottom half of a flat gift box
ruler
pencil
construction paper
scissors
liquid white glue
sea shells, driftwood, sea glass, beach stones,
    coral or other natural things

Let's Begin

1. Paint the inside of the box with blue or green poster paint.
2. Make a center wall for the inside of the box from a strip of construction paper as long as the longest side of the box. Add a little more paper to the length on both ends of the strip to make fold-over tabs, Fig. a.
3. Fold back the paper tabs on both ends just enough so that the center wall fits perfectly in the box, Fig. b.
4. Squeeze liquid white glue onto the outside of each tab.
5. Place the wall in the center of the box, and press the tabs to the sides, Fig. c.
6. Make cross walls from strips of construction paper cut as long as the distance between the side of the box and the center wall. Add extra paper on each side of the strips for tabs.
7. Fold and glue the cross walls into the box just as you did with the center wall. You can glue as many cross walls as you wish into the box making compartments of whatever size you wish.
8. Glue your beach treasures into the small windows with liquid white glue.
9. You can hang your dried collage on the wall using string or a stick-on picture hanger.

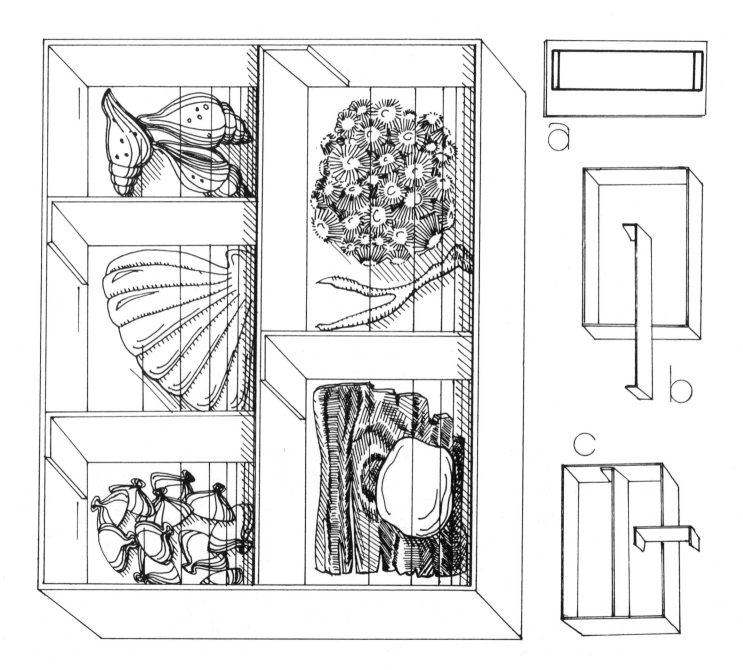

a

b

c

Shell Comb

No matter where you are, you carry a creature that is all mouth and no body. It's your hungry comb with more teeth than a baby shark. Hair is the only food that will satisfy its appetite. If your comb is rather dull-looking, then it's time to give it a face lift, and decorate it with tiny shells. Collect or buy small shells to decorate the top of your comb. You probably won't want to carry this comb with you all the time, since some of the shells might come off. If you have a comb, brush, and mirror, you can glue shells onto all three items and have a matching set.

Things You Need

comb
liquid white glue
small sea shells

Let's Begin

1. Start with a washed comb or buy an inexpensive one at the store.
2. Squeeze liquid white glue on the band above the teeth of the comb. Cover the entire top of the comb.
3. Let the glue dry for several minutes.
4. Place small shells on top of the glue. Some can face up and some down. Make your own design. Let it dry thoroughly before use.

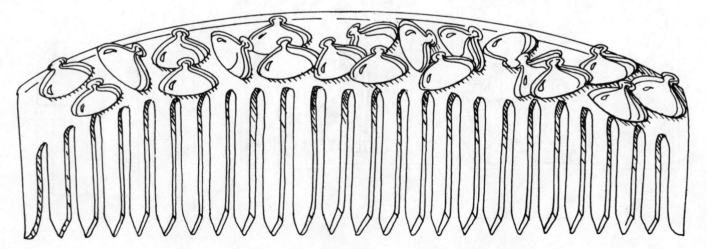

Sand is
a blanket
by the sea

Sand is a blanket by the sea

Dipping your burning toes in the cool ocean is a real treat on a hot, sunny day at the beach. The sand can get very hot unless it is chilled by the rushing waves. Even when it is hot, sand has a soft, silky touch that feels good when you run your fingers or toes through it. Billions upon billions of tiny rocks, shells, and other natural things have been ground fine to create this soft, sandy blanket. It is nice to lie on, bury yourself in, or build a sand castle with. If you dig a hole deep enough in the sand, you will find the ocean at the bottom of it.

Sand has many craft uses. The projects in this chapter will prove to be very interesting. Did you know that you can make a plaster sunburst using sand as a mold or dry flowers in it? Well, you can. You can also dye sand and pour it in different colored layers into jars and glasses, creating beautiful patterns. If you've never constructed a sand castle at the beach, all of the directions for making one are given. It is true that the best place to find sand is by the ocean or in the desert. Don't worry, however, if you live inland or in the city. Sand is available in hardware and hobby stores where it is sold by the bag. Everyone, no matter where they live, can have the pleasure of creating projects with sand. By making the crafts that follow, the thrills of the beach can be yours all year long.

Super Sand Castle

Imagine crossing over a moat filled with hungry crocodiles and entering a castle as large as a football field. What excitement there must have been when kings, queens, counts, and princesses ruled the world. If you had lived hundreds of years ago and were lucky enough, you might have been a Knight of the Roundtable or a princess or a king.

There aren't too many castles to live in these days, but you can do the next best thing by building one when you go to the beach or neighborhood sandbox. Why not bring some play soldiers with you when you go to make this very special fortress?

Things You Need

scissors
colored construction paper
liquid white glue
toothpicks
shoe box
coffee can
funnels
small pail
soup can
sand

Let's Begin

1. Sometime before your trip to the beach or neighborhood sandbox, cut triangles from colored construction paper.
2. Using the liquid white glue, glue the triangles to the toothpicks for flags.
3. Take the flags, shoe box, coffee can, funnels, and soup can with you to the beach or sandbox.
4. Use the wet sand that is near the water if you are at the beach. (Take a gallon of water with you if you are going to build your castle in a sandbox)
5. Fill the shoe box with wet sand.
6. Turn the box upside down onto the flat sand.
7. Unmold the sand by carefully lifting up the box.
8. Fill the cans with wet sand.
9. Turn the cans upside down, the larger one at the side of the shoe-box-molded sand, and the other at the end of it, see illustration. Carefully, lift the cans.
10. Fill a small pail with wet sand and carefully turn it upside down on top of the shoe-box-molded sand. Lift the pail.
11. Fill a funnel with wet sand and carefully turn it upside down on the pail-molded sand. Do the same on the coffee-can molded sand.
12. Add the paper flags to the castle as shown in the illustration.
13. Make windows in the castle by poking holes carefully into the sand with your finger.

Sand-Casted Sun

The sun is very important to every living creature and plant, and without it the earth would be colder than your freezer (in fact, there would be no life on earth without the sun). If you have ever seen fanciful drawings of the sun, you will notice that sometimes it is shown smiling and sometimes not. This sand-casted sun has a happy face. Put it in your room, or give it to someone you like as a very pretty present.

Things You Need

large gift box
aluminum foil
sand
pie tin
plastic spoon
plaster of paris
coffee can
paper clip

Let's Begin

1. Line the bottom and the sides of a gift box with aluminum foil. Be careful to get the foil into the corners.
2. Scoop sand into the box.
3. Sprinkle water onto the sand so that it is wet enough to make a hole if you poke your finger into it.
4. Smooth the sand evenly in the box.
5. Press the bottom of a pie tin completely into the sand, Fig. a. Don't press beyond the rim.
6. Carefully lift the pie tin from the sand. You should have created an impression of the bottom and sides of the pie tin in the sand.
7. Make a face design on the bottom of the impression with your fingers, Fig. b.
8. Poke a design into the side of the impression with your fingers, Fig. b.
9. Stirring all the while, mix plaster of paris and water in the coffee can until it looks like loose whipped cream.
10. Quickly spoon the plaster into the impression in the sand, Fig. c.
11. Smooth the top of the plaster with the back of a plastic spoon.
12. Open a paper clip, Fig. d.
13. Push one end of the open clip into the plaster near the top of the sun, Fig. e.
14. The casting will dry very slowly because of the wet sand. In ten days, remove your casting and hang. (To speed up the drying, place the box of sand in the sun.)

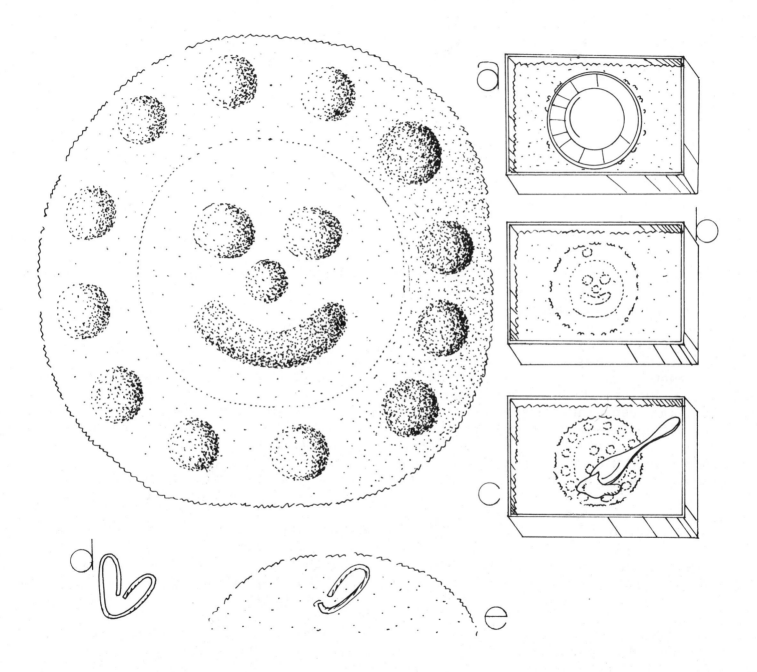

Fantasy Sculptures

Have you ever imagined that you were someone else living in a different time? If you have, then you have been in the world of fantasy. There are no real things in a fantasy (though the fantasy seems and is very real). Everything is designed in the halls of your imagination. You create the characters, the setting, and the story. These sculptures are fantastic because they come from your imagination and can be whatever you want them to be: animals, plants, or just strange things. Here is a craft that can be enjoyed anytime you feel like a little fantastic daydreaming.

Things You Need

plastic spoon
plaster of paris
coffee can
sand
waxed paper
poster paints
paintbrushes
sequins

Let's Begin

1. Stirring all the while, mix water and plaster of paris in a coffee can until it looks like cream.
2. Quickly stir enough sand into the plaster of paris to make the mixture look like thick whipped cream. Work fast, because the plaster dries quickly.
3. Pour some of the plaster mixture from the can onto a piece of waxed paper creating towering squiggles, Fig. a.
4. Spoon the remaining plaster out of the can in long creations, Fig. b.
5. Squeeze the tall squiggles to create unusual designs. Do this quickly before the plaster hardens.
6. When the sculptures have dried, paint and decorate them using poster paints and sequins, and remove from waxed paper.

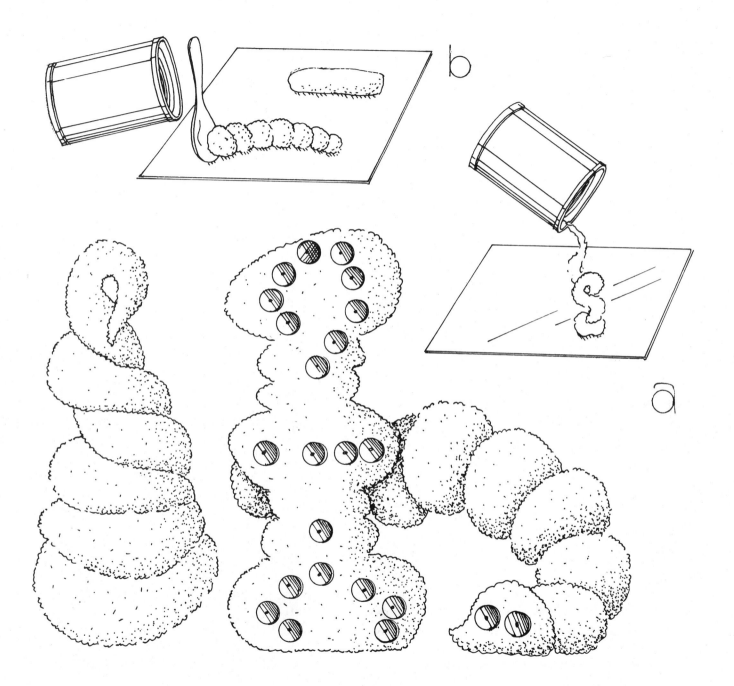

b

a

Apple Pin Cushion

"An apple a day keeps the doctor away," but if you bite into this one you may find yourself the not-so-happy recipient of a house call. You'll get a mouth full of sand! The Apple Pin Cushion is a gift Mom may have wanted for a long time. Pins and needles get lost very easily. When they are placed in this apple, the sand will hold them in place until it's time to sew the hole in your sock or that tear in your pants. If you like to sew, then you might want to make an Apple Pin Cushion for yourself.

Things You Need

scissors
scraps of red and green felt
needle and thread
plastic wrap
tablespoon
sand
rubber band

Let's Begin

1. Cut two circles from red felt, Fig a. They should be as large as the finished apple illustration.
2. Cut a leaf shape from green felt.
**3. Thread a needle.
4. Place the leaf between the two felt circles, Fig. b.
5. Start to sew the two circles together at the leaf shape with a small running stitch, see the directions given in Bean Bags, page 114.
6. Sew small, tight stitches halfway around the edge of the circle, Fig. c. Leave the threaded needle in place in the middle of your sewing.
7. Cut five large squares of plastic wrap.
8. Place the squares on top of each other.
9. Spoon three tablespoons of sand on top of the wrap stack, Fig. d.
10. Gather the ends of the plastic wrap around the sand, and twist rubber band tightly around the gathered wrap, Fig. e.
11. Trim the gathered wrap with scissors, Fig. f.
12. Place the bag of sand between the two red circles of felt, Fig. g.
13. Let gathered end of the wrap stick out from the circles near the green leaf. This will be the stem.
14. Finish sewing the circles together, Fig. h.
15. Sew the last stitch several times to form a knot before you cut away the thread.

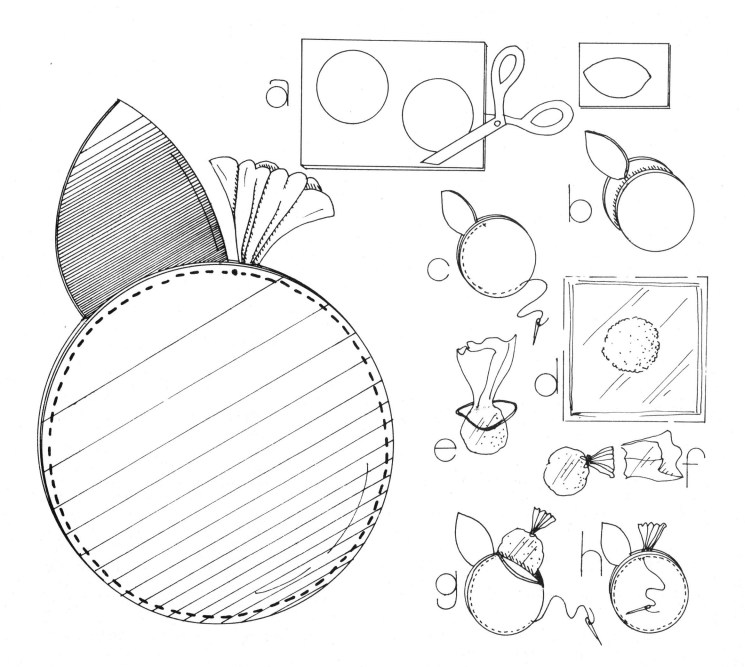

Bubble Bird Cage

Most of our flying feathered friends could not live in a bird cage. They must live and eat outdoors. There are several types of birds that can be kept in a cage: parrots, parakeets, and finches. You may already have a pet bird, but nothing like the caged creature you will make in this project. If you look at the illustration, you will wonder how it is made. The secret is using a balloon, but you will have to read further to unlock the mystery.

Things You Need

round balloon
string
colored yarn
liquid white glue
paper cup
waxed paper
paintbrush
sand
straight pin
tracing paper
pencil
scissors
yellow construction paper
paper punch

Let's Begin

1. Blow up a round balloon.
2. Knot the neck of the balloon, or tie it closed with a piece of string.
3. Tie a length of yarn to the neck of the balloon.
4. Wrap the yarn around the balloon in all directions, Fig. a.
5. After wrapping, tie the loose end of the yarn to the neck of the balloon.
6. Pour liquid white glue into a paper cup.
7. Place the yarn-wrapped balloon on a sheet of waxed paper.
8. Paint all of the yarn with liquid white glue.
9. Sprinkle sand evenly onto another sheet of waxed paper.
10. Roll the balloon over the sand to coat the yarn completely with sand, Fig. b.
11. Let the yarn dry thoroughly.
**12. Break the balloon with a straight pin.
13. Carefully peel away the broken balloon from the inside of the yarn.
14. Trace the bird shape from the book onto tracing paper. Cut out the tracing.
15. Using the tracing as a pattern, draw the bird on a sheet of yellow construction paper.
16. Cut out the bird and draw an eye on it.
17. Punch a hole in the bird's head with a paper punch or with the point of the pencil.
18. Tie yarn through the hole on the bird.
19. Tie the bird in the cage, see illustration.
20. Tie yarn to the top of the cage for hanging.

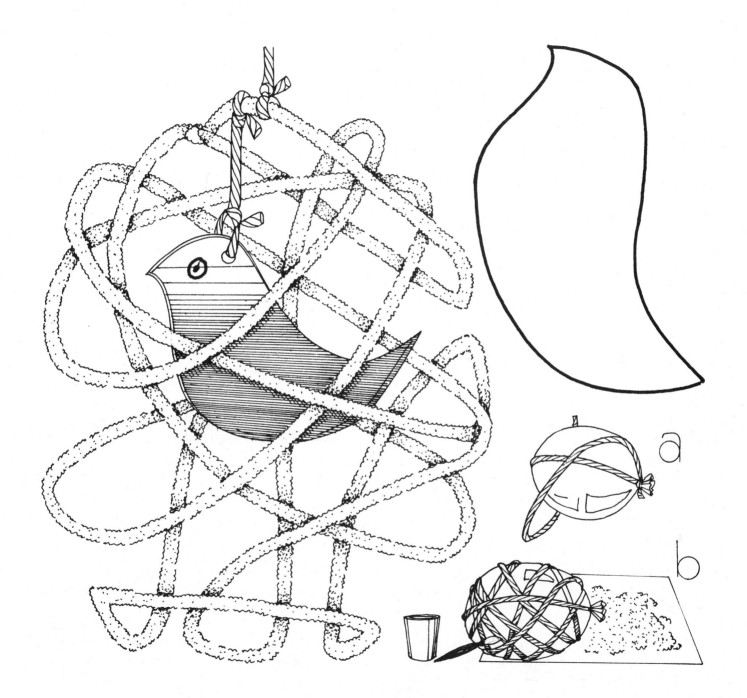

a

b

Sand Pouring

Sand pouring may not sound very interesting to you, but when the sand is colored, you can make many beautiful objects with it. Collect several small jars with lids, and bring home a bag of sand the next time you are at the beach. Once the sand is dyed, start making different colored sand layers in the jars. You can use these sand-poured jars as paper weights or as decorations in your room.

Things You Need

paper cups
fine sand
powdered fabric dyes or food coloring
plastic spoons
paper towels
small jars with lids
paper clip

Let's Begin

1. Fill paper cups half-full with sand.
2. Add water to each cup to cover the sand completely.
3. Add different colors of powdered fabric dye or drops of food coloring to the water and sand. The more coloring you add, the deeper the color of the sand.
4. Stir the sand, water, and dye with a plastic spoon, Fig. a.
5. Let the sand sit in the dye and water for fifteen minutes.
6. Pinch the edge of the cup so you can pour out most of the water without spilling the sand. Pour out the water.
7. Spoon the sand from each cup onto separate sheets of paper toweling, Fig. b. Keep colors separate.
8. Spread out the sand and let it dry.
9. Spoon a layer of colored sand into a small jar which you have washed and dried well, Fig. c.
10. Carefully spoon different layers of colored sand on top of one another into the jar, Fig. d. The last layer should barely come to the neck of the jar.
11. Open a paper clip to form a straight piece of wire.
12. Holding the wire against the inside of the jar, push the wire down through all the layers of sand, Fig. e.
13. Pull the wire out of the jar and you will see how it pulls the different layers into each other.
14. Make these designs around the entire jar.
15. When the design is finished, spoon sand to the top of the jar and screw on the lid, Fig. f.

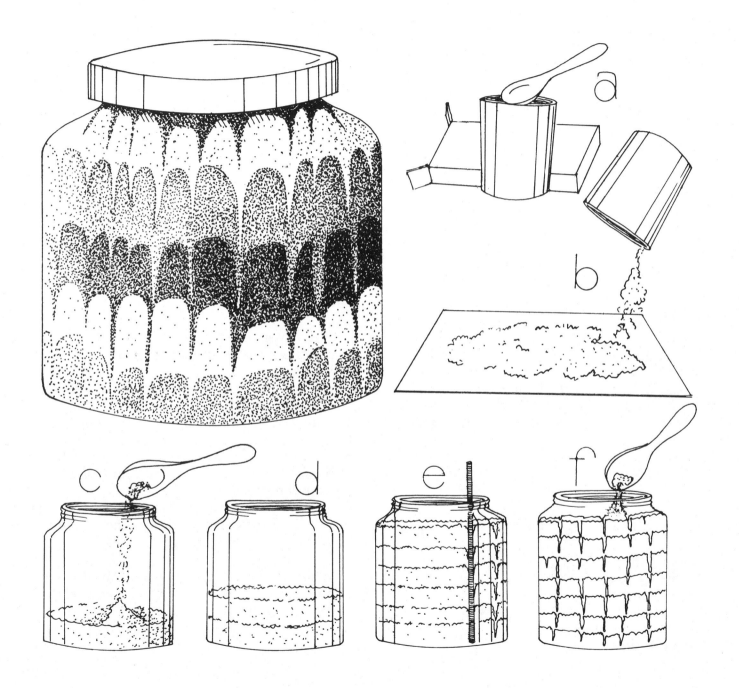

Sand Painting

Because sand can be dyed any color, it can be used to create beautiful paintings. As an artist uses paint on a canvas, you will use colored sand. The subject for this sand painting is a butterfly and an apple on a branch. Find pictures of these natural beauties, and decide what colors to dye your sand. Once you start working on this painting, you won't be able to put it down.

Things You Need

pencil
heavy white drawing paper
sand
paper cups
boxed dyes or food coloring
plastic spoons
paper towels
liquid white glue
paintbrush

Let's Begin

1. With a pencil draw the design shapes as you see them in the illustration on a sheet of heavy paper, Fig. a.
2. Dye and dry the sand as described in Sand Pouring, page 190.
3. Pour liquid white glue into a paper cup.
4. Using the paintbrush, fill in one of the design shapes with the glue, Fig. b.
5. Sprinkle one color of dyed and dried sand over the glued area, Fig. c.
6. Repeat gluing design shapes and sprinkling on different colored sand in different areas of your design.
7. Let the painting dry.
8. When the painting has dried, tip it over a paper towel to remove any excess sand that did not glue in place, Fig. d.

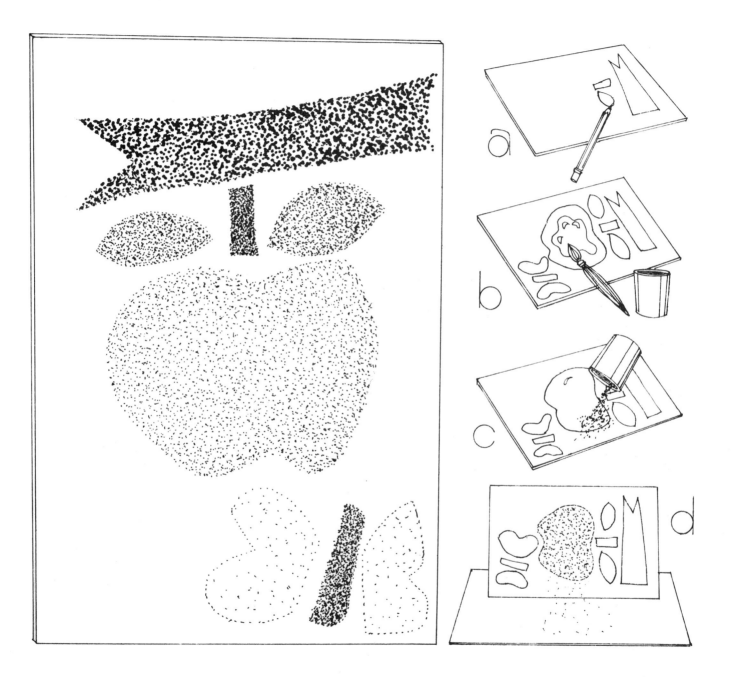

Sand Dried Flowers

There is always a need for a bouquet of lovely flowers. The bouquet you will make will consist of dried flowers—flowers with soft colors that last a long, long time. Gather flowers from the fields or from your garden, and start drying them immediately. Once you have dried enough flowers, start making bouquets and garlands for every room in your home.

Things You Need

cardboard box
sand
scissors
freshly picked flowers
drinking straws or florist sticks
beading wire (purchasable in five-and-ten-cent stores) or pipe cleaners
green construction paper
liquid white glue

Let's Begin

1. Fill the cardboard box half-full with sand.
2. Cut away most of the stem from each flower. The remaining stem should be as long as your middle finger, Fig. a.
3. Push the stem of each flower into the sand, Fig. b.
4. Sprinkle a thin layer of sand over the flowers making sure to cover them completely, Fig. c. If you have a thick flower with many petals, such as a rose, open the petals slightly, and fill in the spaces between the petals with sand.
5. Place the box in a dry place like a closet or an attic.
6. Let the flowers dry in the sand for two weeks.
7. When the flowers have dried, carefully tilt the box and pour out the top sand.
8. Carefully lift out the flowers.
9. Florists sell green wooden sticks that can be used as stems for your flowers. You can also use drinking straws. Carefully attach flowers to the stems with beading wire or pipe cleaners, Fig. d.
10. Cut out leaves from green construction paper.
11. Glue the leaves to the stems of the flowers.

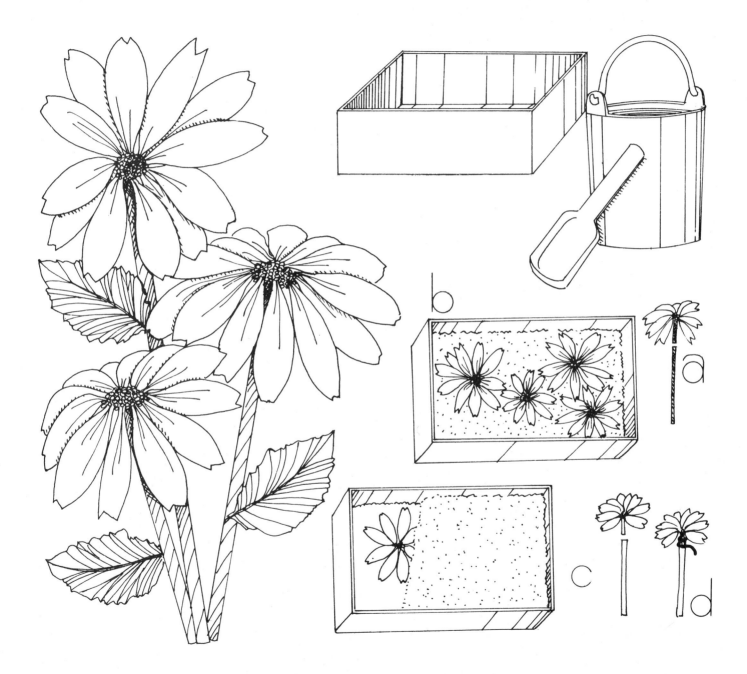

Cactus Terrarium

A terrarium is a closed container in which small plants or animals live in a controlled atmosphere. You won't be using small animals for this project, just cactus plants. Have Mom or Dad buy one or more cacti, then find a jar large enough to contain them. Add a rock or rocks to this glass-enclosed, desert. Add some water when you cannot see moisture beads on the inside of the glass jar. Your cactus terrarium will be a treasure that will seem to draw you into its miniature environment.

Things You Need

large jar with a lid
sand
small cactus plants
tiny rocks
hammer and nail

Let's Begin

1. Wash and remove the label from a large jar.
2. Add sand to the jar.
3. Plant small cactus plants in the sand.
4. Add some pretty rocks.
5. Sprinkle just enough water into the jar to wet the sand.
6. Screw on the lid.
**7. Make small holes in the lid with a hammer and nail.

Fruit is
a beautiful
sweet

Fruit is a beautiful sweet

You know you like candy, but what about fruit? Both contain sugar—that's probably the big attraction. But though candy may come first when you want something sweet, there are times when nothing but fruit will do. Think of a cold crunchy apple or a sweet and sloppy slice of watermelon. We say that fruit is nature's candy, but it is so much more. Take a good look at a peach or a bunch of grapes sometime. You'll never see such a beautiful candy bar. Fruit's a beautiful sweet—to your eye and hand as well as your sweet tooth.

You are probably wondering why there is a chapter on fruit in a craft book. Many interesting things can be made with fruit. Most fruits required for the projects here can be obtained easily at the supermarket. If you enjoy outdoor adventure, however, you may want to hunt for fruit yourself. Blackberries, raspberries, and blueberries grow in most parts of the country during the summer. Don't look for berries in the forest, however. They grow where the trees end and the fields begin. They will be useful when you want to make berry ink.

Since fruit is available at the store all the time, have Mom or Dad buy only that amount you will need for the crafts you intend to make right away. Unless you use (or eat) the fruit immediately, it will spoil. And speaking of eating, try to refrain from ingesting your craft materials or your project will very much lack something. Although that orange would be delicious, you're going to be out a beautiful and fragrant pomander ball!

Caramel Apple Friends

You don't have to travel very far to enjoy a good caramel apple. All it takes is a bag of caramels, a bowl of apples, and some funny face-making assorted candies. Your Caramel Apple Friends will be amusing—not to mention—delicious companions.

Things You Need

two saucepans, one larger than the other
small tin can
1 package vanilla caramels
spoon
jelly apple sticks
4 to 6 apples
candies, sprinkles, coconut
waxed paper
cookie sheet

Let's Begin

1. Fill the larger saucepan half-full with water.
2. Place a small tin can upside down in the water.
3. Put the smaller pot on the can in the larger pot, Fig. a.
4. Add caramels to the smaller pot. (Do not use the chocolate fudge that are sometimes packed with the caramels.)
****5. Place the saucepan arrangement on top of the stove and turn the burner on to a medium heat. Stir the caramels with a spoon until they melt. You can also melt caramels in a single saucepan directly over a low heat. If you do, add a teaspoon of milk and stir constantly.
6. Push a jelly apple stick into the top of a washed and dried apple.
****7. Dip the apple into the melted caramel, coating it by swirling it in the melted caramel, Fig. b. Be sure that the entire apple is covered with caramel.
8. Hold the apple by the stick and make silly faces with candy trimmings. Work fast. The following are instructions for making the caramel apple faces:
Face A. Use chocolate sprinkles for hair, gumdrops for eyes and nose, and string licorice for the mouth.
Face B. Use chocolate chips for hair, chocolate-coated dots for eyes and nose, and an orange slice for the mouth.
Face C. Use coconut for hair, sourballs for the eyes, and red hots for the nose and mouth.
Face D. Use string licorice for hair, candy wafers for the eyes, and miniature marshmallows for the mouth.
9. Place the decorated apple upside down on a sheet of waxed paper placed on a cookie sheet, Fig. c.
10. Spoon remaining caramel onto waxed paper. Press the caramel flat, to make caramel candy drops.

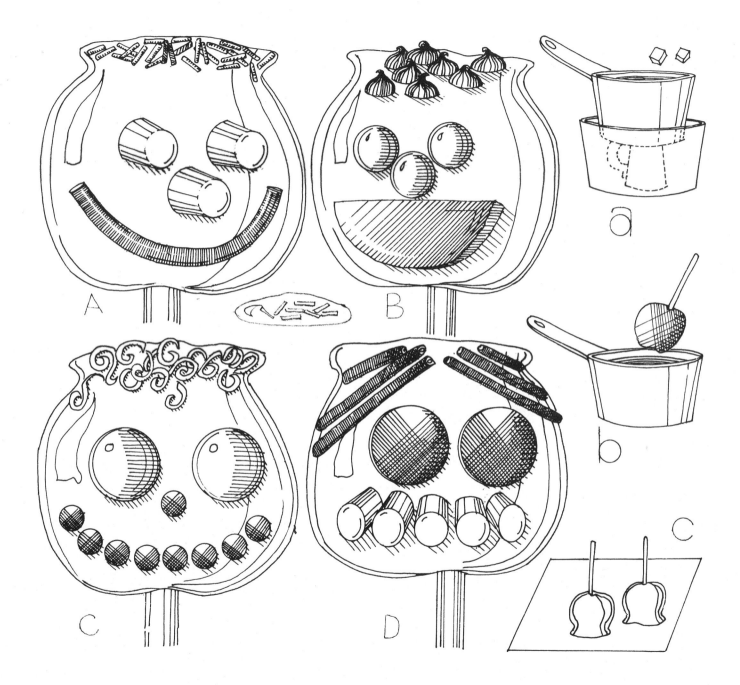

A

B

C

D

a

b

C

Apple-Head Puppets

Did you know that apples make wonderful puppets? You create the costumes for the puppets and decorate the apple heads to make funny faces. Choose apples that aren't too perfect for this project because you won't be able to eat them after the puppet show is finished.

Things You Need

apples
spoon
toothpicks
miniature marshmallows, gumdrops or grapes
cotton napkin or handkerchief
3 rubber bands

Let's Begin

1. Remove the stem from an apple.
**2. Scoop out a deep hole in the top of the apple with a spoon, Fig. a.
3. Break toothpicks in half.
4. To make faces, push the toothpick halves through miniature marshmallows, gumdrops, or grapes and then into the apple.
5. Place a cotton napkin or handkerchief over your hand as shown in Fig. b.
6. Wrap and twist a rubber band not too tightly around the three extended fingers as shown in Fig. c.
7. Push the hole in the apple head over the top (middle) finger. The two side fingers work as arms. Make as many puppets as you wish, but give each a unique candy face.

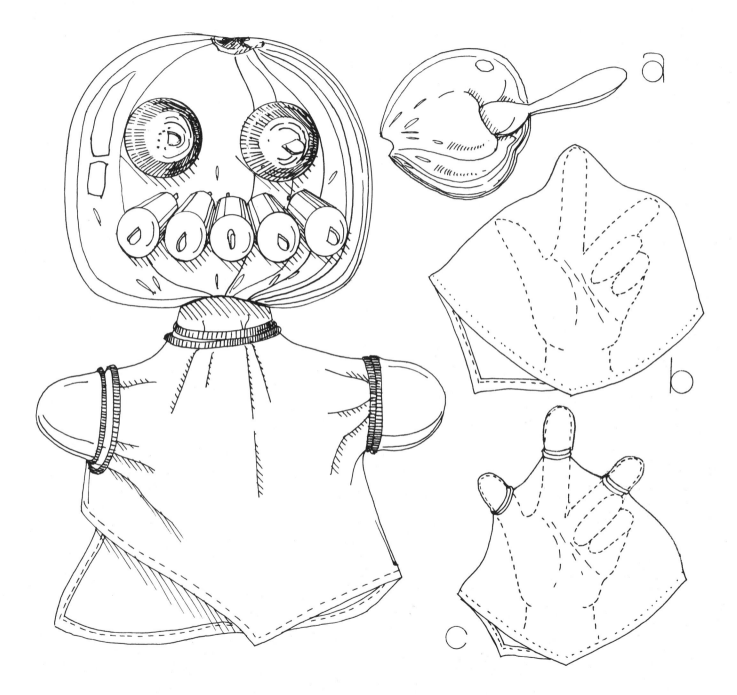

a

b

c

Fruit Printing

Have you ever cut a piece of round fruit in half? If you have, then you know that the exposed surface has a pretty design. Every fruit you cut in half reveals a different pattern. You can use cut fruit to make prints. Get yourself a stack of paper and a bowl of fruit, and experiment with different fruits and colors. Once you have mastered fruit printing, you can make beautiful prints for your room.

Things You Need

knife
apples, oranges, lemons
poster paints
paper plate
paintbrush
white drawing paper

Let's Begin

**1. Cut a piece of fruit in half, Fig. a.
  2. Pour a little poster paint into a paper plate. Spread it evenly over the bottom of the plate with a paintbrush, Fig. b.
  3. Press the cut side of the fruit into the paint.
  4. Lift the fruit from the plate.
  5. Press the painted fruit onto white drawing paper. Be careful not to move the fruit as you print, Fig. c.
  6. Carefully lift the fruit to see the print.

a

b

c

Orange Pomander Ball

People have always placed sweet-smelling things in their drawers or closets to make them smell especially fresh. The most popular freshener is the sachet bag filled with dried lilac. Another old-fashioned closet sweetener is the orange pomander ball. Pioneer women used this spicy-smelling ball to remove unpleasant odors from the kitchen. You will want to have a pomander ball in your room as Mom or Dad will undoubtedly want one for their closet or dresser drawers.

Things You Need

whole cloves
orange
cinnamon
plastic bag
ribbon or netting
string

Let's Begin

1. Push the pointed stems of whole cloves into the skin of an orange, Fig. a. Cover the entire orange with cloves, see illustration.
2. Sprinkle cinnamon into a plastic bag.
3. Place the orange in the bag, Fig. b.
4. Hold the top of the bag as you shake the orange in the cinnamon.
5. Remove the orange from the bag.
6. Tie a length of ribbon around the orange and knot it, Fig. c.
7. Tie a second ribbon criss-crossing the first ribbon at the bottom, and knot at the top.
8. Tie a length of string around the knotted ribbons.
10. Hang the ball in a special place. The orange will eventually shrink in size and become hard, but should not lose its scent.

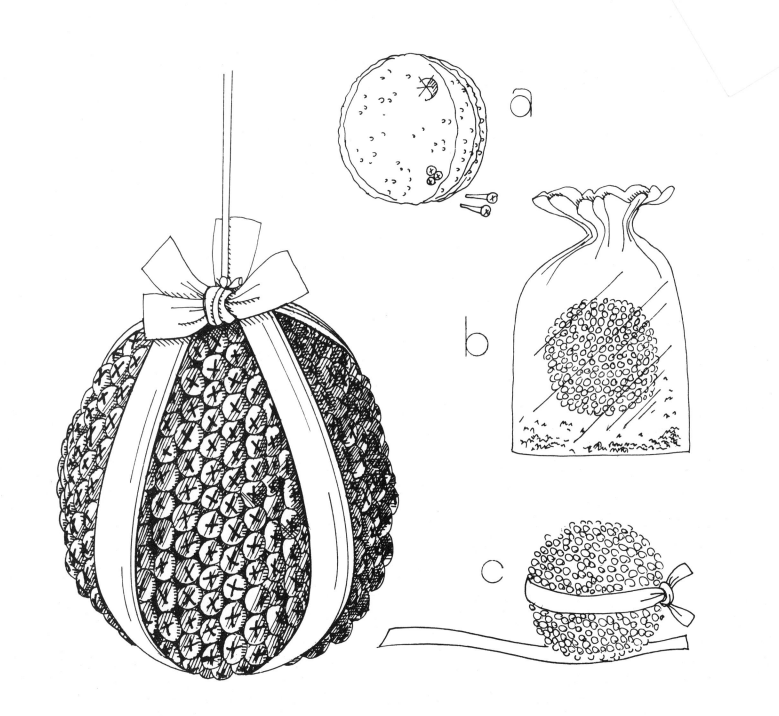

a

b

c

Pear People

Pears are fruit with a shape that may remind you of a person sitting on the floor. Now all you need to add is a face, arms and legs. With everything in place, your pear person will entertain you and your family enormously.

Things You Need

fresh pears
toothpicks
grapes
knife
maraschino cherries

Let's Begin

1. Stand a pear upright on its wide bottom.
2. Make two arms and two legs by pushing two grapes onto each pick, see illustration.
3. Push the toothpicks into the pear for the arms and legs.
**4. Cut a maraschino cherry in half with a knife.
5. Break a toothpick in half.
6. Push each half toothpick through each half of the cut maraschino cherry.
7. Insert the maraschino cherry halves into the pear for eyes. You may make many pear people for a funny bowl of fruit.

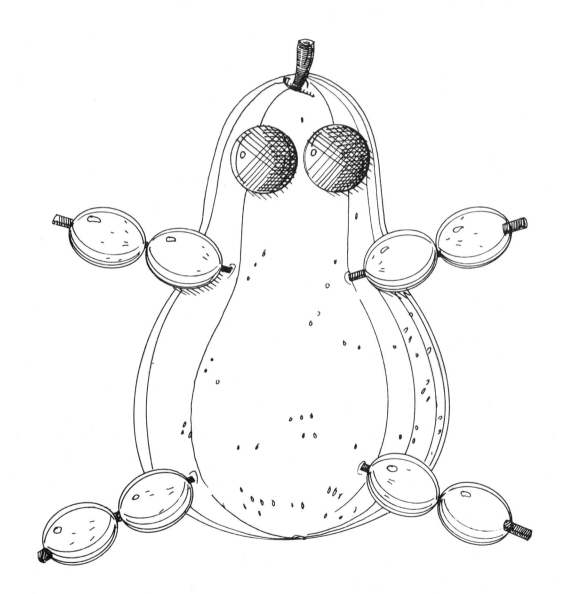

Canned Fruit Animals

If you like what's inside a closed can of fruit, then you'll love what you can do with the contents once the can is open. You can make all of your favorite animals from canned fruit. And you get to eat them for a fabulous dessert.

Things You Need

spoon and spatula
canned pineapple slices, peach halves, apricots, and pears
paper towels
small paper plates
cake decorating gel in a tube

Let's Begin

1. Spoon out the canned fruit onto paper towels. Blot the fruit until it is dry.
2. Use a spatula to lift the fruit onto a small paper plate.
3. Make the animals as described below:

LION: Place a peach half on top of a pineapple slice. Use cake decorating gel to draw a lion face on the peach half.

MONKEY: Use a pear half and add apricot halves for ears. Draw a monkey face on the pear with cake decorating gel.

RABBIT: Use a peach half for the face. The ears are made from peach slices. Draw on a face and ear design with cake decorating gel.

BEAR: Use a peach half for the face and add apricot halves for the ears. Draw on a face with cake decorating gel.

For serving, animals can also be placed on a slice of pound cake or a dish of jello.

Berry Ink

When you write a letter to a friend or to your grandparents, you probably use a ball-point pen. Before the ball-point pen was invented, people used a fountain pen that contained ink or a stick pen that had a point which was dipped in ink. It is very tiresome dipping a pen continuously into ink, but if you've never written in this way it could be fun. You will enjoy writing even more if you make your own ink. All you need is some ripe berries and something to crush them with. Believe it or not, this was one of the ways writing ink was first produced.

Things You Need

ripe cherries, blueberries, blackberries or
   strawberries
small jars with lids
spoon
paper towels
paper cups

Let's Begin

1. Remove stems and leaves from ripe berries and place them in a small jar.
2. Press the berries to a pulp with the back of a spoon, Fig. a.
3. When the berries are crushed, add a little water. The more water you add, the lighter the color of the finished ink will be, Fig. b.
4. Stir the mixture well, Fig. c.
5. Place a sheet of paper toweling over a paper cup. Push the paper towel down into the cup, Fig. d.
6. Slowly pour the berry mixture through the towel in the cup, Fig. e.
7. Let all of the liquid drain through the towel. Remove the towel and throw it away.
8. Pour the strained ink back into the jar and screw on the lid.
9. Use a straight or fountain pen to write with the berry ink.

a

b

c

d

e

Cranberry Necklace

Almost anything can be strung to make a necklace providing it is small enough. Cranberries are good to use because they are firm and have no pits. They are also quite round and look like large red beads. With the addition of construction paper charms, this necklace will look pretty around your neck. The kids at school as well as the teachers will be amazed at your creation.

Things You Need

needle and thread
scissors

colored construction paper
whole fresh cranberries

Let's Begin

**1. Thread a needle with a long length of thread.
  2. Cut small charm shapes from colored construction paper.
**3. String cranberries onto the thread using the needle. Alternate berries with paper charms, see illustration.
  4. Knot both ends of the string of cranberries to form a necklace.

Even you can love vegetables

Even you can love vegetables

How many times have you heard that awful command, "Eat your vegetables, they're good for you!" Well, they are, but they can also be delicious. It may take a while to like vegetables, but once you do, you really do. A sweet and buttery ear of corn, tender peas served, perhaps, in a little cream, even spinach—properly prepared—these vegetables could make you forget the meat and dessert. No, you won't *have* to eat any vegetables to tackle this chapter (this is not a cookbook), but you may learn to love them if only by making wonderful crafts that use them.

Unless you have a vegetable garden, all the vegetables you will need will have to be freshly bought. If they have been in the house for days or weeks, they may be too old to use. One of the projects in this chapter calls for a potato as a printing press. If the potato you use is not firm, it will be hard to carve designs into it. In order to make a carrot necklace, you must have a hard carrot. If you don't, the individual carrot beads will droop on the string.

Look through the chapter and see what vegetables you will need for the crafts you want to make. Go shopping for them with Mom or Dad. After you complete your projects, you may want to sample some of the "raw materials" yourself. Even you can love vegetables—as mouth-watering craftwork or simply beautiful eating.

Carrot Necklace

Carrots are supposed to be good for your eyesight. They can also do wonders for your neck. Wonders for your neck? Yes, if you turn them into a pretty orange necklace. Carrots can be sliced and strung on a string to create a most unusual piece of neckware. Be very careful, however. Don't wear your necklace in the vicinity of a hungry rabbit!

Things You Need

large carrots
potato peeler
knife
string or dental floss
needle with a large eye
typewriter paper

Let's Begin

1. Scrape the outside of a carrot with the potato peeler, Fig. a.
**2. Cut the carrot into medium-sized slices, Fig. b.
**3. Thread the needle with enough string or dental floss to go over your head when the necklace is completed.
**4. Thread the carrot slices by pushing the needle through the center of each slice, one by one, Fig. c. Leave a little space between each slice as you thread.
5. Tie the ends of the string together to close the necklace.
6. Lay the necklace on a sheet of paper, Fig. d.
7. Place the paper in a dry place, such as a closet or in the attic so that the necklace can dry completely.
8. Your necklace should be ready to wear in ten days.

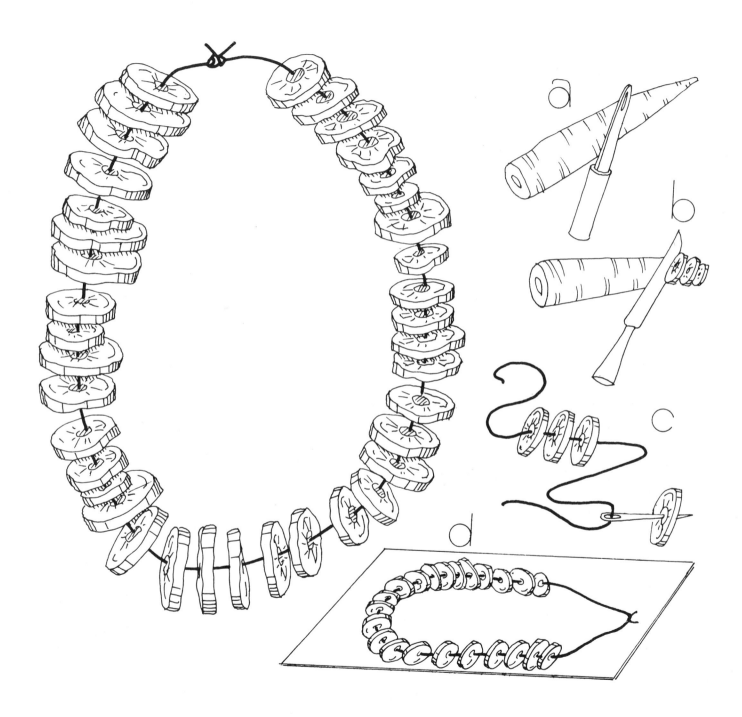

a

b

c

d

Colored Celery Tree

Have you ever wondered how a tree gets water from the soil? It's not too difficult to understand. Water first enters the roots that are in the ground. From the roots, the water travels up "tubes" in the tree all the way to the top of the branches. Every branch and leaf is nourished through these tubes. If there is no moisture in the ground, the tree will die.

If you want to see this process for yourself, this project will help you do it. You will need water, a stalk of celery, and two different colored food dyes. Do this project in the evening, or just before you go to bed. When you wake up in the morning you will see that your celery stalk has absorbed the dyed water and that the leaves have changed colors.

Things You Need

knife
celery stalk with leaves
2 drinking glasses
boxed dyes or food coloring (2 colors)
spoon

Let's Begin

**1. Trim away part of the bottom of the celery, Fig. a.
**2. Slice halfway through the center of the celery stalk with a knife, Fig. b.
3. Fill two glasses at least three-quarters full with water.
4. Add a different color of dye or food coloring to the water in each glass. Mix well with a spoon. Add enough dye to make a very strong or dark solution, Fig. c.
5. Place the two glasses next to each other. Slip one end of the cut celery stalk into one glass and the remaining end into the other glass, see illustration.
6. Let the celery remain in the dye overnight. In the morning, the different dyes will have traveled up the celery stalk and the leaves will have colored beautifully.

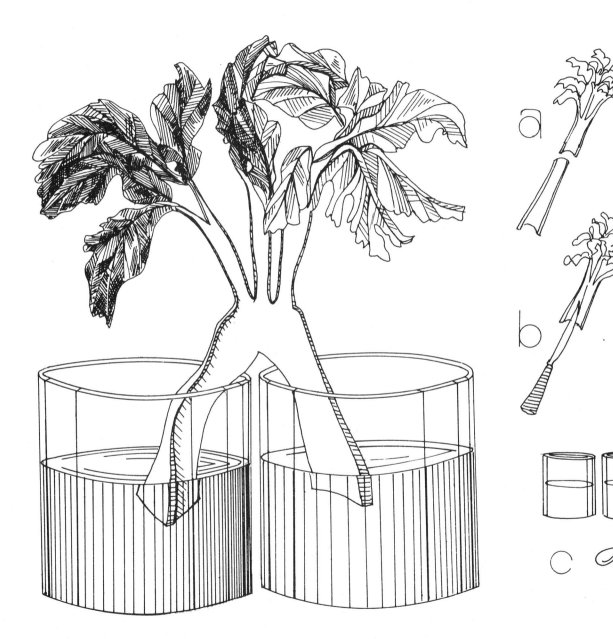

a

b

c

Painted Pumpkins and Gourds

A favorite Halloween craft is the decoration of pumpkins and gourds. Fall is actually the only time of the year you can do this because pumpkins and gourds are harvested then. Even if it is not the jack-o-lantern season, you can still think of unusual faces and designs to paint on a gourd or a pumpkin. Hold onto your ideas, and when the right season arrives, get ready to make this craft. Place the completed projects behind your front door or on your window sills to keep the Halloween spirit at your very own house during this spooky time of year.

Things You Need

pumpkins and gourds
mild soap
poster paint or model airplane enamels
kitchen cleanser
paintbrush

Let's Begin

1. Wash pumpkins and gourds with mild soap and water. Let them dry completely.
2. Mix a little kitchen cleanser to poster paints in small paper cuts. You can also use model airplane enamels.
3. Use oil-base paints to create a wonderful assortment of autumn friends, see illustration for examples.

Popcorn Painting

The Indians were probably the first to enjoy a tasty bowl of popcorn. They would dry the kernels and save them for popping during the winter and spring months. If it weren't for the Indians, you probably wouldn't be able to munch on a bag of buttered popcorn while watching a horror movie.

Popcorn can be dyed and used in many creative projects. Why not try your hand at a popcorn painting? You can make a lovely flower that will add a delicious touch to your room.

Things You Need

pencil
white drawing paper
popping corn
cooking oil
pot with lid
paper cups
food coloring
spoon
paper towels
liquid white glue

Let's Begin

1. Draw a simple design on a sheet of paper such as the one you see in the illustration.
**2. Have Mom or Dad pop some corn for you. Follow the instructions which come with the popping corn.
3. Fill cups with water and add different colored food coloring to each one.
4. Add a few popped corn kernels into each of the colors, Fig. a.
5. Stir the kernels once and quickly remove them from the cups with spoon. Place them on a paper towel to dry, Fig. b.
6. Let the colored popped corn dry completely.
7. Fill in an area of your design with liquid white glue. Place one of the colors of the dried popped corn on the glue.
8. Glue and fill in all of the areas of your design using a different colored corn for each area.
9. Let the popcorn painting dry overnight.

a

b

Artichoke Flowers

Have you ever eaten a flower? If you like to eat artichokes, then—guess what—you have eaten one of nature's edible flowering plants. Artichokes are the unopened flowers of a thistle-like plant. Thistle plants produce a purplish blossom and have many thorns. You might find them growing wild along the highways in the country.

Artichokes, like other vegetables, can be dried. Since they resemble flowers, the dried plants can be included in a bouquet of dried flowers, or placed in a vase by themselves. Artichokes are a seasonal vegetable, so you will have to check with the grocery store to see if they are being sold.

Things You Need

pencil
artichoke
cotton
poster paints
paintbrush

Let's Begin

**1. Push a sharpened pencil into the base of an artichoke, see illustration.
2. Stuff cotton between some of the leaves of the artichoke.
3. After a few days the artichoke will begin to dry slightly. Push more cotton between as many leaves as you can.
4. The artichoke leaves will be tightly arranged, but as the artichoke dries, insert more cotton, between the leaves. When the artichoke has been stuffed with as much cotton as possible, let it dry completely. The drying time will differ, depending on what part of the country you live.
5. When the artichoke has dried, remove all of the cotton that is between the leaves.
6. The artichoke flower can now be painted with poster paints. If you have spray paint in a can, use this, but let Mom or Dad help.

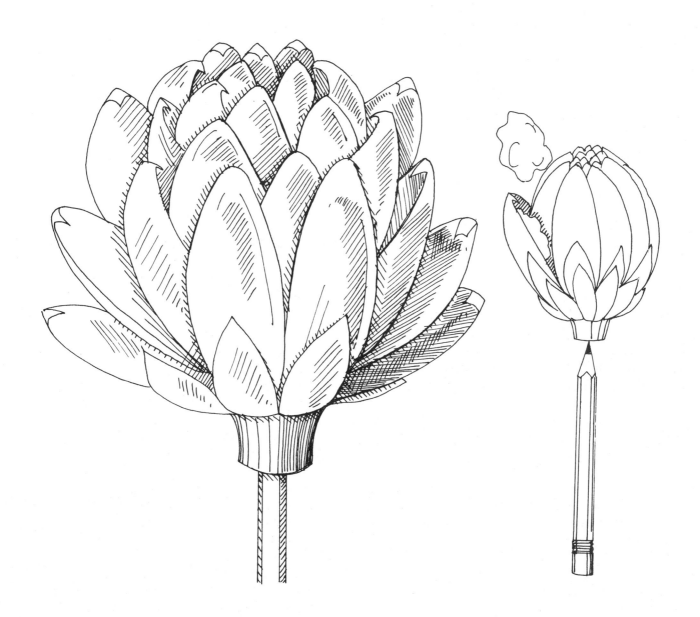

Potato Face

There is a vegetable that has more eyes than you do but can't see a thing. Do you know what it is? It's the brown-skinned potato. Of all the vegetables cooked in your home, the potato is probably the one you like the most. Shoe-string, mashed, french-fried, scalloped—these are some of the many potato preparations you have probably tasted. All of them are delicious, each in its own special way.

Potatoes grow in every shape imaginable. Some are round, some are long, and some are twisted. No matter what the shape, you can design a hundred different faces for it. Use your imagination to make a clubhouse of potato-face pals.

Things You Need

tracing paper

pencil
scissors
colored construction paper
toothpicks
large potato

Let's Begin

1. Using a pencil, trace all of the features from the book onto a sheet of tracing paper.
2. Cut out the features from the tracing paper.
3. Place the tracing paper cutouts on colored construction paper and trace around them.
4. Cut out the features from the colored construction paper.
5. Break toothpicks in half.
6. Push a toothpick through a paper feature and then into the potato.
7. Create a different look by adding a hat, glasses, or a mustache.

Potato Printing

To make a potato print, you carve a design on the surface of a cut potato, paint it, and press the painted design onto a piece of paper. What you get is an impression with an interesting texture. Even the largest potato doesn't have a very wide surface once it is cut in half, so you will probably want to repeat a single design in interesting ways all over your paper. The design in the illustration is of a three-leaf clover. Your print could show a bouquet of clover or clover prints arranged in an interesting scattered design. Create your own potato printer design, print it on the things that belong to you. Potato printing is a lot of fun, especially on days when you have to stay indoors.

Things You Need

knife
potatoes
paper towels
water-color felt-tipped markers
potato peeler
poster paints
paper plate
paintbrush
paper

Let's Begin

**1. Cut a large potato in half, Fig. a
  2. Blot moisture from the potato's surface with a paper towel.
  3. Draw a simple design on the potato's surface with a colored felt-tipped marker, Fig. b.
**4. With a potato peeler or knife, scoop away the part of the potato that surrounds the drawn design, Fig. c. The design should be raised above the potato's surface.
  5. Pour a little poster paint onto a paper plate.
  6. Spread paint over the plate with a paintbrush.
  7. Either press the potato into the paint or brush the paint directly onto the design, Fig. d.
  8. Press the painted potato design onto a piece of paper.
  9. Lift the potato carefully to see your print, Fig. e.

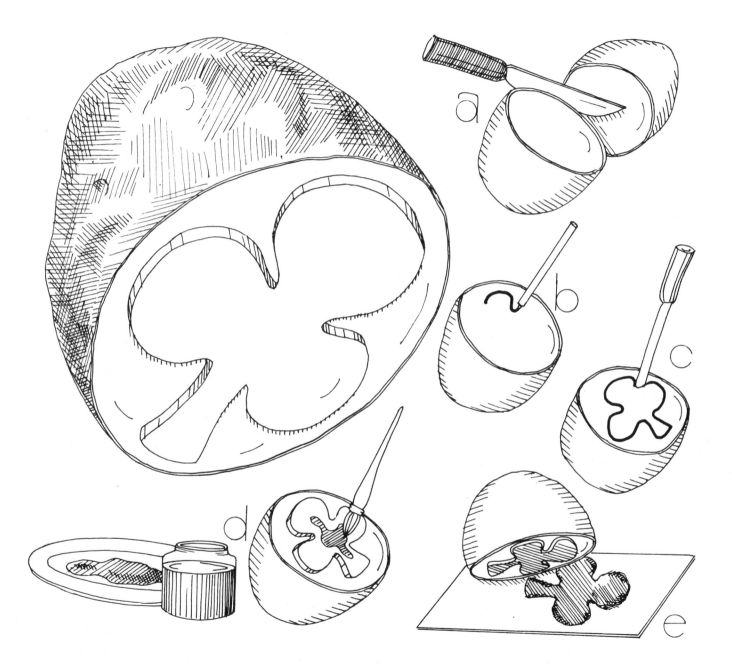

a

b

c

d

e

Sweet Potato Plant

When you plant a seed, you never get to see what is happening below the soil. It takes one to two weeks before the green shoot breaks through the surface of the dirt. Now you can watch the entire growing process by planting a sweet potato in a glass. You will see the roots grow first and then watch a beautiful, leafy plant sprout out of the potato top.

Things You Need

toothpicks
sweet potato
glass

Let's Begin

1. Push four or more toothpicks halfway into a sweet potato. They should be inserted in the bottom third of the potato, see illustration.
2. Place the potato in a glass with the toothpicks resting on the top rim.
3. Pour water into the glass. Make sure the end of the potato is in the water.
4. Place the glass on a window sill or any place where it will get a good deal of light. It will take a few weeks before you see roots growing out of the sides and bottom of the sweet potato. Keep the water level in the glass constant. Soon purplish sprouts will grow from the top of the potato.

5. You can leave the plant in the glass, or pot the sweet potato in soil, as you wish.

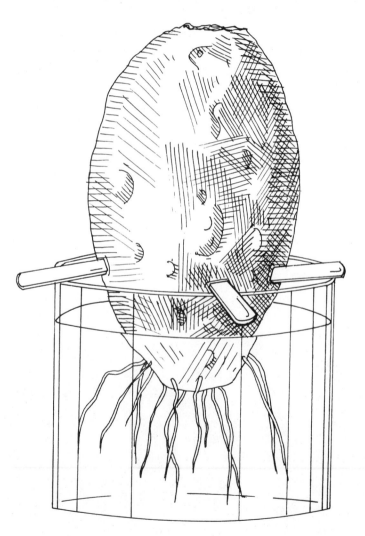

Nature is filled with wondrous things

Nature is filled with wondrous things

Nature is all around you. Even if you live in a large city, nature in the form of birds, bugs, and buds live with you. In the country it is easy to locate natural wonders. All you have to do is head for the nearest tree. It's not quite that simple in the city, but if you look carefully, you will surely find something "natural" to delight you. It might be a weed growing through the crack of the pavement outside your apartment. It might be a sparrow nesting in a hole in a brick wall. You might even see a spider web stretched across a corner of the ceiling in a little-used room.

Of course, natural things and their products are used by people every day no matter where they live. Did you know that things like sugar, salt, feathers, and bones are all part of nature? We have been using natural materials for craftwork, and this chapter should take us even further in this special enjoyment of them. We will use the rain to produce fascinating prints, a sponge's surface to make a lunar landscape, a wishbone for a good luck necklace. There are so many wonderful moments in this chapter, it's time to get started right away. Perhaps you'd like to begin with a craft that uses everyday sugar in a new way—to make a "mountain" of rock candy you will find delicious to eat.

Feathered Peace Pipe

The Indians smoked a peace pipe as a gesture of love and understanding with their fellow tribesmen and the settlers of the Old West. Perhaps you could use one after playing a particularly hard game, or whenever you think things might be better for a little calm and quiet.

Things You Need

small paper cup
red construction paper
pencil
scissors
liquid white glue
red glitter
drinking straw
feathers

Let's Begin

1. Turn a small paper cup upside down on a piece of red construction paper.
2. Trace around the rim of the cup with a pencil, Fig. a.
3. Cut out the traced red circle.
4. Stand the cup up on its base.
5. Push a pencil through the center of the cup on an upward angle, and out through the opposite side, Fig. b. See the dotted line in the illustration.
6. Using liquid white glue, glue the red circle onto the top of the cup. Fig. c.
7. Spread some glue over the top of the red circle.
8. Sprinkle red glitter over the glue, Fig. d.
9. Push the straw through the two holes in the cup. Let a little of the straw poke through the other end, see illustration.
10. Glue the straw in place.
11. Glue large feathers to the straw.

a

b

c

d

Salt Play Clay

You know how much fun it is to get a package of clay and mold strange creatures from it. Did you know that you can make a non-messy clay in your own kitchen? All of the ingredients you will need for it can be found in the cupboard. You will probably need Mom's or Dad's help with this project. For being so helpful, why not make them a play-clay pendant or medallion.

Things You Need

measuring cup
flour
salt
old saucepan
food coloring
spoon
waxed paper
rolling pin
cookie cutters
plastic drinking straws
scissors
liquid white glue
sequins
yarn
macaroni

Let's Begin

1. Measure one cup of water, one-half cup of flour, and one cup of salt in an old saucepan and mix. Add food coloring if you want to make a colored clay.
**2. Place the saucepan on the stove over a very low heat. Stir continuously.
**3. When the mixture is as thick as rubber, remove the saucepan from the stove.
4. Spoon part of the clay onto a floured sheet of waxed paper, Fig. a.
5. Roll out the clay with a rolling pin, Fig. b. If the clay is sticky, sprinkle with more flour.
6. Cut out designs from the clay with cookie cutters. Punch out a small hole near the top of each cutout with a straw.
7. Roll the scraps of clay into balls.
8. Push the balls of clay onto a plastic drinking straw leaving a little space between each ball, Fig. c.
9. Let the clay shapes and balls dry for a few days.
10. Cut and remove the straw from the balls, which will be used for beads.
11. Using liquid white glue, glue sequins to the cookie shapes.
12. Tie a cookie shape to the middle of a piece of yarn.
13. String the beads on the yarn and tie the ends together.
14. You can make a clay bowl by shaping rolled-out clay with your hands. Press macaroni into the sides before the clay hardens, see illustration.

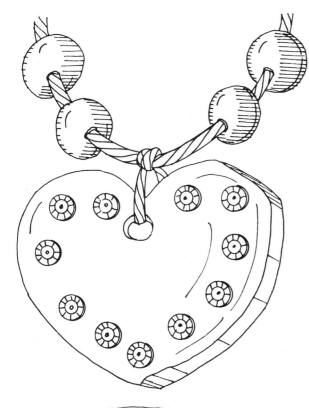

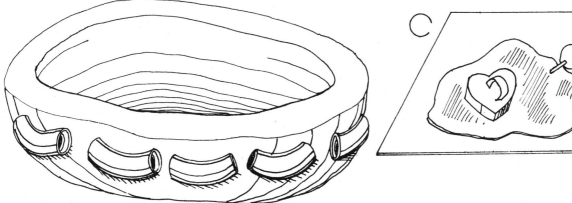

Wheat Sunburst

Wheat is one of the most important plants in your life. If you enjoy eating cereal for breakfast, check out the ingredients on the box. Somewhere between the sugar and the food coloring you should find the word "wheat." All products that contain flour started out as wheat. Some of your favorite food such as cake and cookies are made with wheat in the form of flour.

Wheat is a member of the grass family, and produces a crown of kernels. When wheat turns golden brown, it is time to harvest it. If you can find a field where wheat grows, pick a small bundle. If you can't, it can occasionally be bought at the florist's where it is sold to make dried plant arrangements. Your Wheat Sunburst will make a glorious decoration for your wall.

Things You Need

wheat
waxed paper
liquid white glue
colored yarn

Let's Begin

1. Place an uneven number of wheat stalks in a circle on a sheet of waxed paper, Fig. a. The wheat stalks should overlap one another in the center. They should also be exactly the same distance apart.
2. Squeeze a large dab of liquid white glue onto the overlapping ends of the wheat stalks.
3. When the glue has dried, carefully peel away the waxed paper.
4. Tie one end of a length of yarn to a stalk of wheat near the center of the sunburst, Fig. b.
5. Take the other end of the yarn and weave it in and out of the stalks as if you were weaving a basket.
6. You can tie a different colored yarn to the first as you weave along for a more colorful sunburst. Warm colors, such as yellow, orange, and red, are especially pretty.
7. After you have woven several circles of yarn, tie the end onto the stalk nearest to it. Hang the sunburst on a wall.

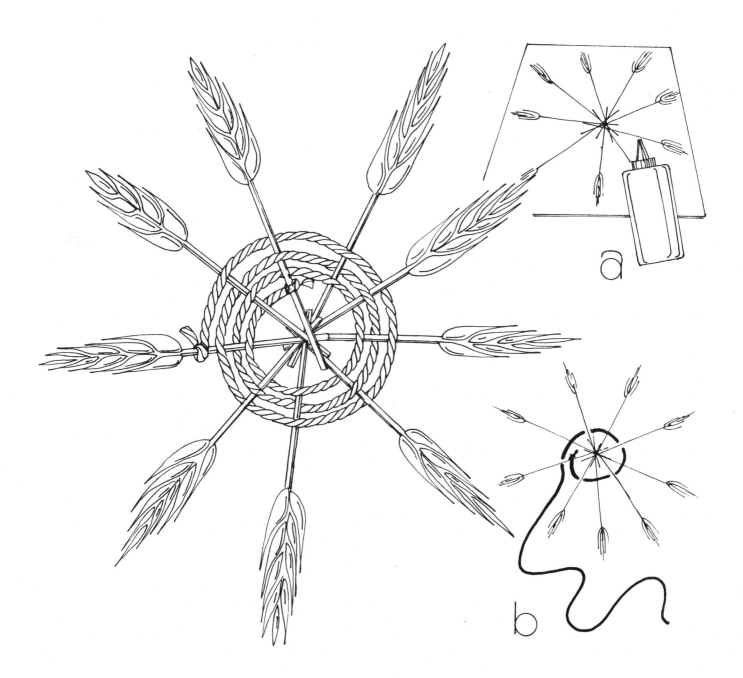

Corn Husk Doll

The Indians were the first to make the corn husk doll. Corn husks were dried, tied, and fashioned into squaws, chiefs, and braves. All additional features were made of corn husk. Faces were painted, and sticks were used to make arms and sometimes legs.

The corn husk doll you will make differs from the original Indian design. This doll is created with yarn, which when properly tied produces all of the parts of the body. Your creativity and imagination will transform these characterless shapes into your favorite storybook figures. Use other materials to create clothing, and glue on facial features.

Things You Need

12 corn husks
yarn, string or cord
scissors

Let's Begin

1. The next time you get fresh corn, save twelve husks or outside "leaves." Gather the husks, and tie them tightly together at one end with the yarn or string, Fig. a.
2. To make the head, tie the husks a little way down from the top knot, Fig. b.
3. Gather three of the husks, and tie them together halfway down for an arm. Gather and tie three more husks, at the opposite side of the doll to form another arm. Cut away most of the excess corn husk that is below the knots, Fig. c.
4. To make the body, tie the remaining corn husks halfway between the head and their ends, Fig. d.
5. Make the legs by taking three husks and tying them together a little up from their ends, Fig. e.
6. Make the other leg the same way.
7. Decorate with colored felt-tipped markers, construction paper, fabric, or any other craft supplies you may have.

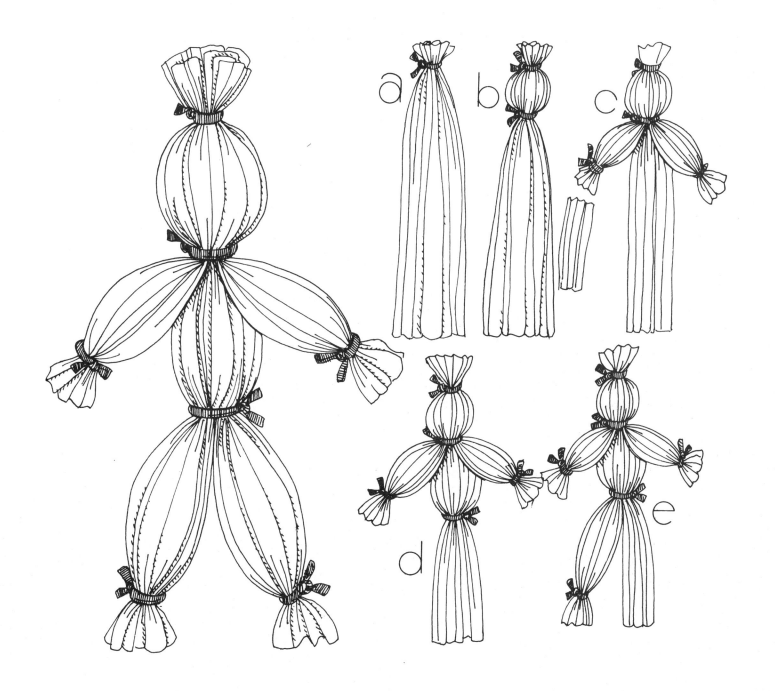

a

b

c

d

e

Sponge Printing

A sponge is a marine animal with a very soft skeleton. It lives in warm, salty water and pretty much stays put on the ocean's floor. Only underwater currents move a sponge from one place to another. People in Europe dive for sponges, and sell them strung on cords like popcorn on streets and in the stores.

People in your house probably use sponges for washing dishes and counters. In most cases these sponges aren't once-alive creatures of the sea. Real sponges are very expensive. The sponges most people use are manufactured. These are flat rather than round, but have pores just like the living variety. Use only flat sponges for this printing project.

Things You Need

colored felt-tipped markers
flat sponges
scissors
poster paint
paper plate
paintbrush
white drawing paper

Let's Begin

1. Draw designs on a sponge with a colored felt-tipped marker, Fig. a.
**2. Cut out the designs with scissors.
3. Spread a little paint on a paper plate with a paintbrush.
4. Dip the cut sponge shape or a chunk of sponge into the paint on the plate, Fig. b.
5. Press the painted side of the sponge onto a sheet of white drawing paper.
6. Carefully lift the sponge from the paper to reveal your print.
7. Let the sponge print dry.

a

b

Sugar Rock Candy

Rock candy looks like precious crystal stones good enough to be strung as glass beads or set in a gold ring band. Only you get to eat these beautiful stones. Open your own sweet shop featuring rock candy hanging like grapes on a vine. By following some simple directions, you can make a little Rock Candy Mountain for your own enjoyment right in your own room.

Things You Need

measuring cup
small saucepan
granulated sugar
spoon
empty glass jar
heavy cord
pencil

Let's Begin

1. Put one cup of water into a small saucepan.
2. Pour two cups of granulated sugar into the water.
**3. Heat the water and sugar on the stove over a medium heat, Fig. a.
**4. Continue stirring until the sugar melts.
**5. Keep adding sugar and stirring until it melts.
**6. Stop adding sugar when you see that it will no longer dissolve in the water. That is, until you see sugar lying on the bottom of the saucepan.
**7. Remove the pot from the stove.
8. Let the liquid cool until it is just warm.
9. Pour the liquid into a clean glass jar.
10. Tie one end of a piece of heavy cord around the middle of a pencil.
11. Place the pencil over the top of the glass jar letting the cord fall into the liquid, Fig. b.
12. Crystals will begin to form in a few hours, Fig. c.
13. The next day, remove the cord from the jar.
**14. Pour the sugar liquid back into the saucepan, reheat and cool it just as you did before.
15. Pour the liquid back into the jar and reinsert the cord with the crystals into it. More crystals will form.
16. If you repeat this procedure every day, the crystal candy will grow bigger and bigger. When it has reached a size that pleases you, snip off any excess string and enjoy.

a

b

c

Crystal Garden

Natural crystals were formed when the earth cooled down millions of years ago. Now they can be grown in your own home. One of the main ingredients for this project is salt, which is itself a crystal. If you look at it under a microscope, salt crystals look like diamonds. You will find this project one of the more exciting natural crafts in this chapter because you can watch the crystals grow larger day by day.

Things You Need

6 charcoal briquets
disposable aluminum pie or pastry tin
measuring cup
salt
liquid bluing
ammonia
coffee can with lid or jar with lid
food coloring in 4 colors

Let's Begin

1. Place six charcoal briquets in the aluminum pie or cake tin, Fig. a.
2. Measure one-quarter cup of salt, bluing, and ammonia and pour all ingredients into a coffee can or jar. Mix them together.
3. Squeeze or sprinkle different food colors onto four of the briquets, one color for each briquet. Squeeze or sprinkle all four colors onto the fifth briquet. The remaining briquet is not to be colored.
4. Pour the salt mixture evenly over the briquets, Fig. b.
5. Place the tin in a warm place.
6. The crystals will start to grow in a very short time.
7. Mix the same solution of salt, bluing and ammonia in the can or jar and cap tightly.
8. Add some of the solution over the garden every two days to keep it growing.

a

b

Mushroom Prints

Mushrooms are one of nature's most interesting creations. They grow in damp, dark places and can pop up through the ground overnight. They have no roots, no leaves and no flower, but they can be found in bright fiery reds and oranges or in snow-white puffs. Some mushrooms are edible but many more are very poisonous. Don't ever eat a mushroom that you find in the woods. If you like to eat these tasty plants, Mom or Dad will buy them and make a tempting dinner with them.

Mushrooms grow in all shapes, sizes, and textures, each with a very interesting design under the cap or head. You can make a print of this beautiful design on books or as paintings in full color. If you don't live near the woods, have Mom or Dad buy several mushrooms at the food store. If you are lucky enough to have the forest in your back yard, choose an odd-shaped mushroom and start printing immediately.

Things You Need

liquid white glue
paper cup
paintbrush
shiny paper or oaktag
piece of corrugated cardboard
mushroom
straight pins
small bowl

Let's Begin

1. Pour a little of the liquid white glue into a paper cup and add just a drop or two of water. Mix with a paintbrush.
2. Place a piece of shiny paper or oaktag on a sheet of corrugated cardboard.
3. Break off the stem from the cap of the mushroom, Fig. a. You may want to remove some of the outer edge of the cap if it hides too much of the gills on the underside.
4. Paint a circle of glue on the center of the paper. The circle should be a little larger than the mushroom, Fig. b.
5. Press four straight pins into the outer rim of the mushroom.
6. Hold the mushroom over the glued area. Do not let the mushroom touch the glue.
7. Press the pins through the paper and into the corrugated cardboard, Fig. c.
8. Quickly place a bowl over the mushroom, Fig. d.
9. Remove the bowl twenty-four hours later.
10. Carefully lift the mushroom off the paper to see the print, Fig. e.

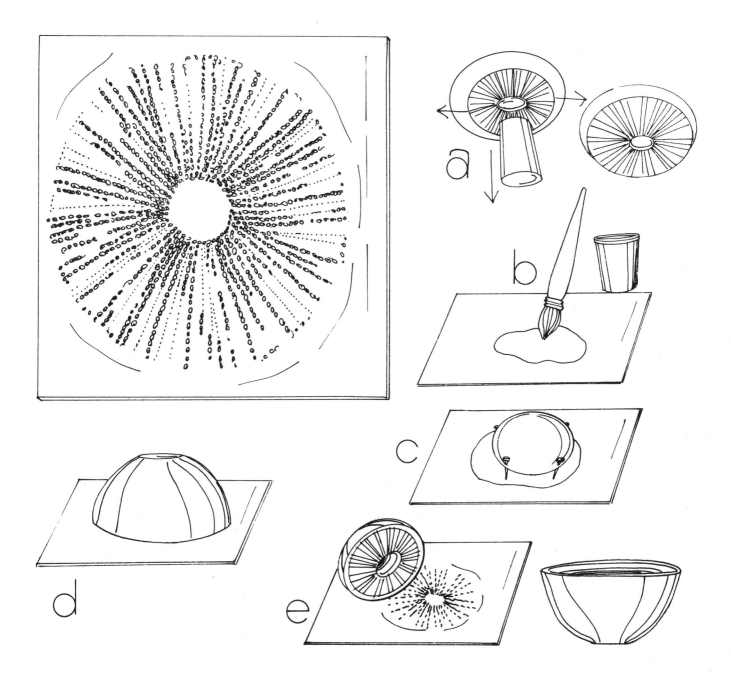

a

b

c

d

e

Web (Printing) Painting

The spider weaves his web to catch insects for a tasty dinner. The web has a sticky surface which holds a bug entangled in it. Try as it might, the trapped insect must wait for the hungry weaver to claim its catch. Only the spider can climb this circular ladder with a thousand rungs.

A spider web is very beautiful, but unless moisture or the rays of the sun strike it, you will probably pass it by. Sometimes you walk right into a web, and how uncomfortable it is having those silky strands dance about your face! Webs are so hard to see because they are so thin. On your next trip into the forest, bring a can of spray paint and a piece of paper with you. The following directions will enable you to print some of the most beautiful designs in nature's pattern book.

Things You Need

white drawing paper
paint in spray can
spider web

Let's Begin

1. Take a walk in the forest and bring white paper and a can of spray paint with you. Find a spider web. Webs are usually found between branches of bushes or between two growing things, such as weeds or garden flowers.
**2. Hold the can of spray paint at arm's length away from the web. Spray quickly with a back and forth motion, Fig. a. Be sure that the wind is blowing away from you when you spray paint so you won't breathe in any of it. Cover the web with a thin coating of paint. The paint will look like tiny beads on the fine strands.
3. Quickly place a piece of paper on the web. It is better if you curve the paper first in the center of the web and straighten it out very carefully along the sides, Fig. b.
4. Let the web dry on the paper. Your finished print will contain some of the web.

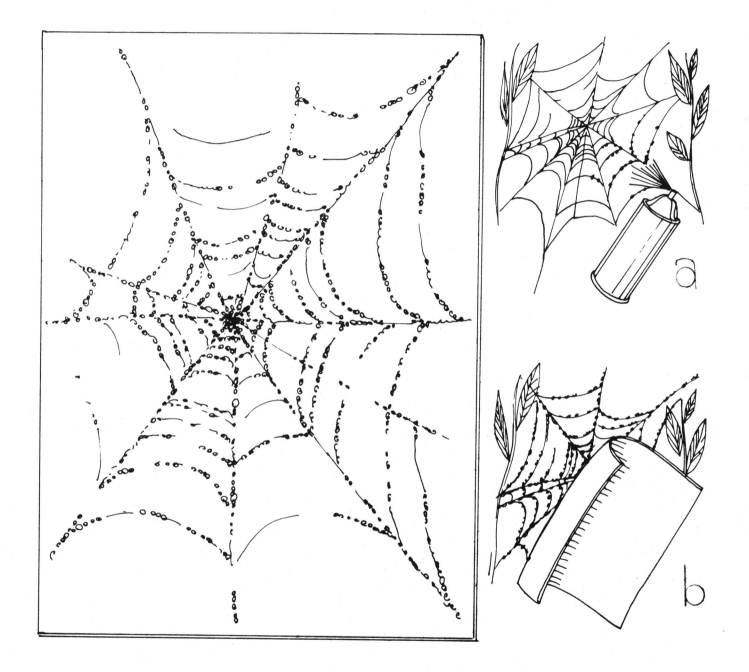

a

b

Rain-Spatter Painting

Here is a project that will make you wish for a rainy day. Are you surprised? Rain-Spatter Painting is so much fun you will do a rain dance every night until Nature rings out her cloudy sponge over your home. All you do is spread paint on a sheet of paper and let the rain create the painting for you. This project can be done by the front door or—with Mom or Dad's supervision—by an open window. If you have to go outside, take your raincoat, umbrella, and boots so that you won't catch a cold. You don't want to spend any of those cloudless days inside in bed!

Things You Need

poster paints

paintbrush
white drawing paper
rain

Let's Begin

1. Paint different colored shapes on a sheet of white drawing paper, Fig. a.
2. When it rains, put the painting outside for just a moment, Fig. b. You might want to wear a raincoat so your arm won't get wet.
3. Take the painting inside. Hold the paper flat so that the drops on the paint won't run.
4. Place the paper on a flat surface, such as a table or the floor.
5. Let the rain dry and see the different patterns it has created.

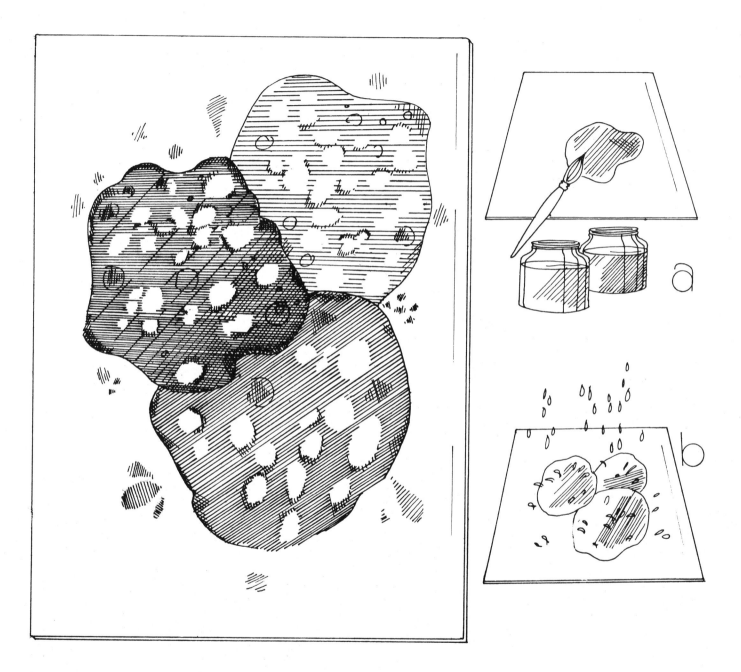

a

b

Two Happy Snowmen

Winter is the season when raindrops fall to earth as fluffy snowflakes. If you are lucky enough to live in a part of the country where snow occasionally covers the ground, then you know how much fun it is to make a snowman. It takes a wet snow to form a really good snowman because it packs very easily. Why not make a really creative snowfriend by adding to it things you have in your home? Make construction paper facial features, wrap an old belt around the snowman's waist, top his head with a cap. No matter how big or small your snowman may be, dress him up in a "Sunday-go-to-meeting" costume. He will be the talk of your neighborhood.

Things You Need

fresh-fallen, wet snow
3 twigs, 2 short and 1 long
charcoal briquets
scissors
colored construction paper
crayons
large belt
paper cups
carrot

Let's Begin

1. Before the snow starts to fall, save three twigs and charcoal briquets and put them in a safe place.
2. Cut a round head and mittens from colored construction paper, see illustration.
3. Draw a face on the head with crayons.
4. Push the two small twigs through the mittens and the long twig through the head.
5. After the snow stops falling, roll a snowball with your hands.
6. Roll the snowball in the fallen snow pushing it into the snow. Continue to roll it until it is large enough for a little snowman.
7. Stick the head and arms into the ball. Add a belt around the middle of the ball, see illustration.
8. To make the large snowman, roll two snowballs, the bottom ball larger than the top ball.
**9. Lift the smaller ball onto the top of the larger ball.
10. Press two paper cups into the head for eyes, a carrot for the nose, briquets for the mouth and buttons, see illustration.
11. Add a hat and scarf.

Wishbone Pendant

What is your favorite part of the chicken? The wishbone, of course! What's it going to be this time: a new toy, a snowy day, or a new pair of pants? No matter what you want, don't break that wishbone! Save it for this craft project. You can make a lucky wishbone necklace. Wear it around your neck, and if you ever need a quick wish, it will be with you at all times.

Things You Need

dried wishbone
cord or yarn

Let's Begin

1. Let a wishbone from a chicken or turkey dry completely.
2. Tie a length of colored yarn or cord at its center around the neck of the wishbone.
3. Tie the ends of the yarn into a knot to make a necklace that will fit over your head.
4. You can paint the wishbone with poster paint or with Mom's nailpolish.

The smooth,
shiny,
slippery stone

The smooth, shiny, slippery stone

In this chapter you will make masks and scenery for an actual three-act play, The *Smooth, Shiny, Slippery Stone,* which is included. You will direct the play and impersonate the characters in it. Imagine having a real show in your own home! Invite your friends over so that they can see the performance. Their applause will tell you how very well you've done.

The play has a message for you. It tells all about how the animals under the Oak Tree try to get rid of something left behind by people after a happy picnic. Luckily, the problem is solved when one of the people—the Little Boy—comes back for it. Had he not returned, the waste object would have remained for a long time, perhaps forever. The idea is, people should try to leave the outdoors clean of litter. Keeping nature free from picnic or other disposables is a way of showing our happiness with our surroundings. If you happen to come across a piece of paper or a tin can in the woods or at the beach, pick it up and toss it into the nearest garbage can. You may not hear a "Thank you!" from a tree, a rock, or a stream, but you can be sure you have done the right thing.

Now that you know the message and what you can do to keep the outdoors clean, it's time to get on with the show! Your performance should help you and your friends learn about nature and how people and nature can live together. It should also be a lot of fun.

Oak Tree and Smooth, Shiny, Slippery Stone

Although the Oak Tree cannot move by itself, the wind can bend and dip its branches. This happens in the Third Act, and makes all the creatures in the forest aware that the Little Boy is approaching.

Things You Need

newspaper
tape
scissors
large fruit juice can
plaster of paris
spoon
green and brown construction paper
paper paste
aluminum foil

Let's Begin

OAK TREE
1. Lay a sheet of newspaper flat on a table or on the floor.
2. Loosely roll the paper at one end to the center crease of the newspaper, Fig. a.
3. Lay a second sheet of paper over the unrolled part of the first sheet of newspaper, Fig. b.
4. Continue rolling newspaper to the center crease of the second sheet of paper.
5. Keep adding new sheets of paper to the center creases, rolling five to ten sheets of newspaper together.
6. Tape the roll together.
**7. Cut four deep slits into one end of the roll of newspaper , Fig. c.
8. Put your finger into the roll, and pull out the center sheet of paper to form a floppy, fringed pole-like tree, Fig. d.
9. Make three fringed poles.
10. Fill a can half-full with plaster of paris. Mix the plaster with water in the can until it looks like heavy whipped cream.
11. Push the three poles into the plaster mixture in the can. Be careful that the can does not tip over.
12. Cut leaves from green paper and paste them to the fringe branches.
13. Cut a piece of brown construction paper as high as the can and long enough to wrap around it. Tape it around the can.

SMOOTH, SHINY, SLIPPERY STONE
1. Make the shiny stone from aluminum foil rolled into a large smooth ball.

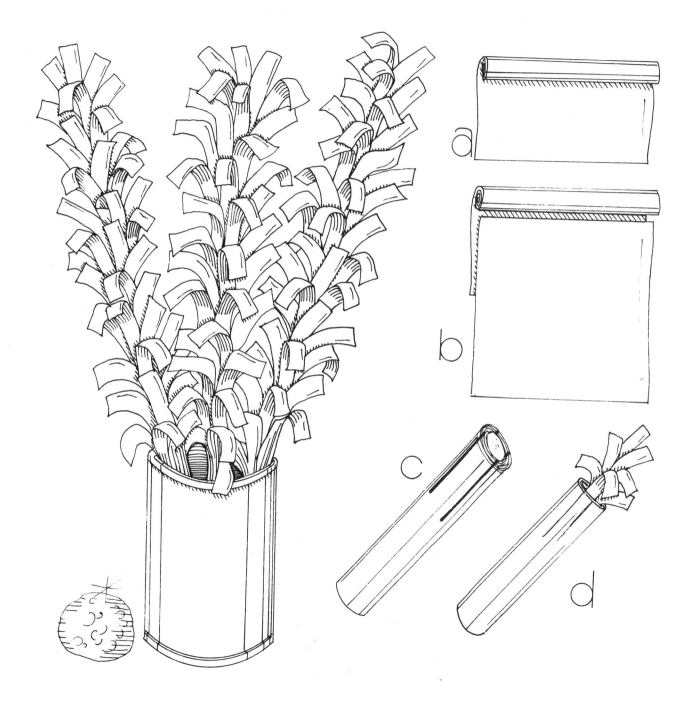

Owl and Molly Mole

In the play, it is Molly Mole who finds herself in trouble. With the aid of her friends, she is freed from the shiny stone that has fallen on top of her home. Owl is the wisest of all creatures, and solves the riddle of the shiny stone.

Things You Need

large brown paper bags
colored felt-tipped markers or crayons
scissors
colored construction paper
paper paste
crepe paper
tape

Let's Begin

OWL
1. Put a bag over your head and feel for your eyes through it. With a crayon, lightly make an X where each eye lies behind the bag. Remove the bag.
2. Cut two large circles for eyes from yellow construction paper.
3. Using colored felt-tipped markers or crayons, draw black circles in the centers of the yellow-paper eyes with short lines around them, see illustration.
4. Using paper paste, paste the eyes on the bag over the Xs you have drawn.
5. Cut a beak and top feathers from colored construction paper, and paste them onto the bag, see illustration.
6. Make the body feathers from long strips of colored paper or crepe paper. Cut slits along one side of the paper, half-way up.
7. Tape or paste each fringe strip to the bag starting at the bottom. Overlap the strips upward to the beak.
8. Cut out two circles through the eyes so that you can see out once you slip the mask over your head.

MOLLY MOLE
1. Mark eyes with an X just as you did for Owl.
2. Roll colored construction paper into a cone and staple or tape it together.
3. Trim the bottom edge of the cone so that it can stand straight.
4. Color the tip of the cone beak using colored felt-tipped markers or crayons.
5. Tape the cone to the bag near the closed end.
6. Cut out two eyes, two ears, a paper bow, and lips from colored construction paper, see illustration. Draw black circles on the center of the eyes.
7. Paste the eyes onto the bag over the Xs you have drawn; paste the other places, see illustration.
8. Cut out two circles through the eyes so you can see out once you slip the mask over your head.

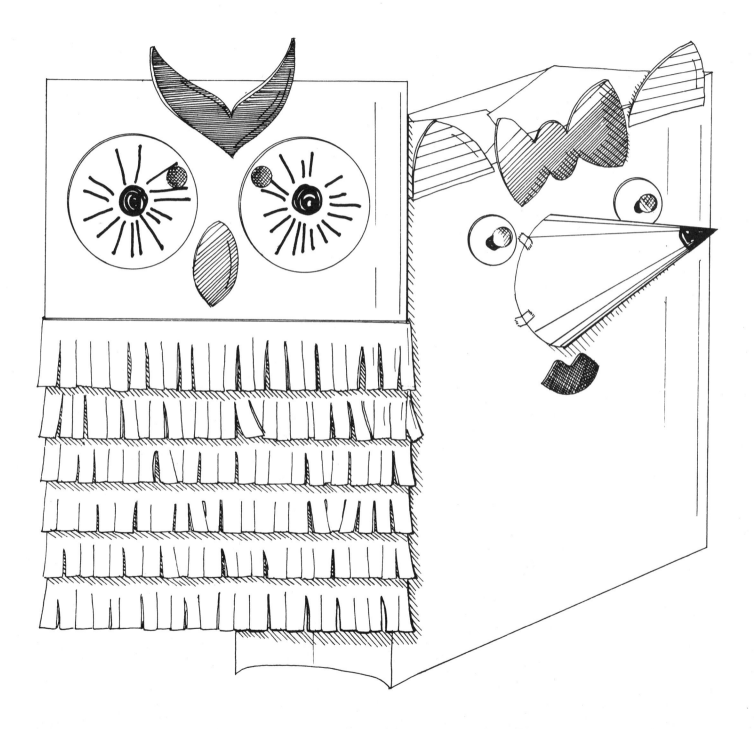

Squirrel and Mr. Turtle

Squirrel is the character who alerts the creatures of the forest to Molly Mole's problem. He is a busy character, always looking for nuts to store away for the winter. Mr. Turtle is the one who drags the shiny stone from Molly's home. (Actually, he would rather spend the day in the pond eating insects and fish.)

Things You Need

large brown paper bag
colored felt-tipped markers or crayons
scissors
colored construction paper
paper paste
drinking straws
tape
cardboard
stapler
yarn or string
oaktag
ribbon

Let's Begin

SQUIRREL

1. Put the bag over your head and feel for your eyes through it. With a crayon, lightly mark an X where each eye lies behind the bag. Remove the bag.
2. Cut out two ears, two eyes, two eyebrows, and a nose from colored construction paper, see illustration.
3. Using paper paste, paste the eyes on the bag over the Xs you have drawn; paste the other shapes on the bag in the proper places.
4. Draw a mouth under the nose with colored felt-tipped markers or crayons.
5. Cut deep slits into one end of both straws.
6. Tape on straw whiskers on both sides of the nose.
7. Cut a bar-like length of cardboard for the tail.

a

b

c

8. Cut two strips of colored construction paper as long as the cardboard.
9. Cut slits along one side of each piece of construction paper.
10. Paste the strips to the cardboard with the uncut edges meeting at the center, Fig. a.
11. Staple the tail to the bottom of the back of the bag, Fig. a.
**12. Using a paper punch or a sharp pencil, punch a hole in the cardboard and two holes in the bag near the top of the back and to one side. Tie a string through the hole in the top of the tail and tie it into the two holes in the bag with a big knot so that the tail swings outward, Fig. a.
13. Cut out two circles through the eyes so you can see out once you slip the mask over your head.

MR. TURTLE

1. Cut out a large oval from a sheet of oaktag. If you can, make the oval from green oaktag.
2. Cut out a six-sided shape from green construction paper and paste it to the center of the oval, Fig. b.
3. Cut out more green paper shapes and paste them around the center shape.
4. Staple a ribbon long enough to go around your waist to the underside of the oval shell, Fig. b.
5. Cut hands and feet like the ones in Fig. c. Use green construction paper.
6. Staple ribbons to the underside of the feet and hands, Fig. c.
7. Tie the shell around your waist, and the hands and feet around your wrists and ankles. To portray the turtle, walk on your hands and feet.

The Smooth, Shiny, Slippery Stone

A play about the forest and the
animals who live there
by Noel Fiarotta

Characters

OWL
MOLLY MOLE
SQUIRREL
MR. TURTLE
LITTLE BOY
OAK TREE

ACT I

SCENE I

Scene: *Morning in the forest. The squirrel's home in the* OAK TREE.

Open Curtain

SQUIRREL (*Yawning, stretching, and covering his eyes with his paws*)
It must be morning! I wish the birds wouldn't chirp so loudly. They wake me up every morning. (*Opening his eyes*) Who turned the lights on! Who?

OWL (*Perched above* SQUIRREL's *home*)
Who! Who! Who!

SQUIRREL (*Looking from the hole of his home. He sees the* OWL)
That's all you ever say.

OWL
I have been awake all night and now I want to get a good day's sleep. Don't make so much noise. I'm sleepy!

SQUIRREL
Why don't you sleep at night like I do?

OWL
I sleep better in the day because I see better at night. It's the only time I can find food to eat.

SQUIRREL
If you are hungry why don't you join me for

breakfast? I have plenty of food stored away. More than enough for next winter.

OWL
Thank you very much, but I would be poor company. I would be asleep before I could get the first acorn to my mouth. *(Yawning)* I'm so very sleepy.

SQUIRREL
Some dark and rainy morning you must eat breakfast with me.

OWL *(Closing his eyes. Mumbling in a sleepy tone)*
Dark . . . rainy . . . morning. Okay. Good day!

SQUIRREL
Good Nighhh . . . t! I mean good day to you. *(Hopping back into his home)* It's so hard getting to know him. He sleeps all day. I think I will eat breakfast under the tree. Maybe someone will join me. *(Looking all around his home)* Now, where did I hide those hickory nuts?

Curtain

Scene: *Under the* OAK TREE.

Open Curtain

SQUIRREL
This looks like a good place to eat breakfast. I guess I will have to eat all by myself. *(Looking around)* There is nobody in sight.

MOLLY MOLE *(From under the ground. In a muffled voice)*
Help! Help! Help! I can't get out!

SQUIRREL
Did I hear someone crying for help? It sounds like it is coming from the mole's home. *(Looking for the* MOLE's *home)* Is that you, Molly Mole?

MOLLY MOLE *(In a muffled voice)*
Yes! Something is covering the entrance to

270

my home. Help me. I don't know if it is a stone or branch.

SQUIRREL (*Looking at the stone and scratching his head*)

I have never seen a stone like this before. It is so shiny. You push and I will pull and maybe we can move it.

MOLLY MOLE (*In a muffled voice*)

I'm pushing as hard as I can.

SQUIRREL

I'm pulling as hard as I can. It is just too heavy for us. Maybe Mr. Turtle can help us. He is walking this way. (*Waving his paw*) Oh Mr. Turtle, can you help us?

MR. TURTLE (*Looking all around*)

Us? I only see one of you. I mean I only see you, Squirrel. Who else might you be talking about?

SQUIRREL

Molly Mole is trapped in her home with a shiny stone rolled over it. We were wondering if you could help us remove it.

MR. TURTLE (*Looking at the stone*)
  With my strength it will be removed faster
  than a rolling acorn. Tie a vine around the
  shiny stone and I will pull it away with my
  teeth.

  (*With the vine in Mr. Turtle's mouth,
  the shiny stone is removed*)

MOLLY MOLE (*Climbing out of her home in the
  ground*)
  Oh thank you very much, Mr. Turtle and
  Squirrel. I thought I would never get out.

MR. TURTLE
  I am glad I could help.

SQUIRREL
  You are lucky Mr. Turtle was walking this
  way.

  (MR. TURTLE, SQUIRREL, *and* MOLLY MOLE
  examine the shiny stone)

SQUIRREL (*Scratching his head*)
  What is it? I have never seen a stone so
  shiny.

272

MR. TURTLE *(Touching it)*
It doesn't feel very hard. It is rather smooth.

MOLLY MOLE *(Also touching the stone)*
It's slippery. It must be a smooth, shiny, slippery stone. But how did it get here?

SQUIRREL
Who placed it here? Who? *(Pause)* Who?

OWL *(Flying down from his branch in the* OAK TREE*)*
Did I hear someone say, "Who?" *(Angrily)* All this noise is keeping me awake. What seems to be the matter?

MR. TURTLE
We are trying to find out who placed this— correct me if I'm wrong Molly Mole— smooth, shiny, slippery stone over her home. *(Looking suspiciously at* OWL*)* Did you roll this stone over Molly's home?

OWL
I did not. I saw everything that happened last night from my branch in the Oak Tree. Nothing strange happened last night. It must have been rolled during the day. Maybe one of you did it.

MR. TURTLE
It could not have been me. I stayed in the pond all day eating insects and fish.

SQUIRREL
I was busy collecting acorns and pine nuts several trees from here. I have to collect extra because sometimes I hide them and forget where they are when winter covers the ground and trees with snow.

MOLLY MOLE
I slept all day long yesterday. Besides, it was my home that was covered by the stone.

SQUIRREL *(Puzzled)*
How can we find out who placed the smooth, shiny, slippery stone over Molly Mole's home?

OWL
By the end of the day we will have the answer. My wisdom will solve this mystery. But first, I must get some sleep. We will meet by the smooth, shiny, slippery stone when the sun moves to the other side of the sky.

*(*MR. TURTLE *goes back to the pond,* MOLLY MOLE *returns to her home in the ground,* SQUIRREL *scampers to his tree home, and the* OWL *goes to sleep on his branch)*

Curtain

ACT II

SCENE I

Scene: *Afternoon in the forest. An important meeting under the Oak Tree.* MOLLY, SQUIRREL, *and* MR. TURTLE *are waiting for* OWL.

Open Curtain

MR. TURTLE
Where is Owl? He is the one who called for a

273

meeting. Did you see him in the tree, Squirrel?

SQUIRREL

I didn't notice. I was in such a hurry to be on time. He is probably still sleeping.

OWL *(Flying to the ground from his branch)*

I am as awake as a fully bloomed daisy on a sunny day. I needed a few more seconds to gather my thoughts.

SQUIRREL

How can you think when you are sleeping?

MR. TURTLE

When I sleep, my head is like the forest at midnight.

OWL

Enough of this chatter. The meeting shall begin. (MR. TURTLE, MOLLY MOLE, *and* SQUIRREL *sit together in front of* OWL(We will start at the beginning. Molly Mole, you will speak first. Tell me everything you remember.

MOLLY MOLE

Yesterday I was gathering food in the early morning sunshine. When I had eaten enough, I crawled back into my home and fell asleep. When I awoke this morning, everything was dark.

OWL

When did you fall asleep?

MOLLY MOLE

Very early in the morning. I don't see too well, but it was shortly after the sun peeked over the trees.

OWL

Did you hear any strange noises during the day?

MOLLY MOLE

I don't hear very well since I spend so much time in the ground. The world was as quiet as a mushroom growing on a damp log. This is all I remember.

OWL

You have helped greatly. We will have the answer when the toads sing their evening lullaby. What do you remember, Mr. Turtle?

MR. TURTLE

I spent all day in the pond eating insects and

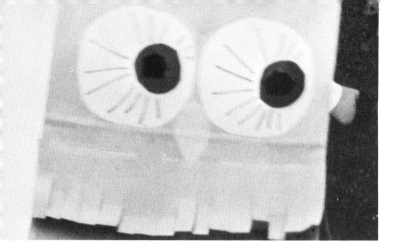

fish. When the sun was shining directly over me, I heard strange loud sounds.

OWL
What kinds of sounds?

MR. TURTLE
The sounds of people talking, yelling, and laughing. I didn't see any people by the pond. It was as noisy as a cornfield of magpies. This is all I remember.

OWL
You have said many helpful words. We will now have the answer before the birds settle down to an evening's rest. And now, Squirrel, it is your task to tell me the missing facts. Think very carefully.

SQUIRREL
I was collecting acorns and pine nuts several trees from here. When I returned in the evening, before the sun set, I saw footprints on a path near the oak tree—big ones, middle-sized ones, and small ones. It looked like a very busy deer path. This is all I remember.

OWL
I am now certain we will have the answer while the sun is in the late afternoon sky. We will have lunch and return when we are full.

(MR. TURTLE, MOLLY MOLE, SQUIRREL, *and* OWL *return to their homes*)

Curtain

SCENE II

Scene: *One hour later under the* OAK TREE.

Open Curtain

OWL
Now that we have eaten, I have some bad news to tell you.

MOLLY MOLE
You didn't find who placed the smooth, shiny, slippery stone over my home.

OWL
More serious than that!

SQUIRREL
Don't keep us waiting. What is it?

MR. TURTLE
Yes, please don't make us wait another minute longer.

OWL *(Very sad)*
While we were busy doing our work, many people sat under this tree. The footprints you saw, and the noise you heard were made by people having a picnic. You were fast asleep, Molly Mole, that is why you didn't hear anything.

SQUIRREL
Then a people must own it and placed it over Molly's home.

OWL
That is correct.

MOLLY MOLE *(Puzzled)*

Then what is the big problem?

OWL
The smooth, shiny, slippery stone doesn't belong in the forest. It should have been taken away with the people who had the picnic.

MR. TURTLE
And now we must get rid of it by ourselves.

MOLLY MOLE
I'm too small to move the stone!

SQUIRREL
So am I!

MR. TURTLE
I could only move it several inches before I get tired.

OWL
With all of my wisdom I can't fly with it in my claws.

ALL
What are we going to do?

OAK TREE *(In a mighty voice)*
I was the only one who saw what happened. It was fun seeing the people having a good time in the forest. It is not fair to us if we

have to live with the things people leave behind.

MR. TURTLE
You are right! It isn't fair.

MOLLY MOLE
Especially when it is dropped on your home . . .

SQUIRREL
. . . and we can't get rid of it.

OWL
Can you help us, Oak Tree?

OAK TREE
No, only the wind can bend my branches. I can only provide food, home, and safety for you, the animals of the forest. This is why I'm here.

OWL
Let us go back to our homes and try to solve our new problem. If anyone can come up with a solution, wake me up.

(MR. TURTLE, MOLLY MOLE, SQUIRREL, *and* OWL *return to their homes)*

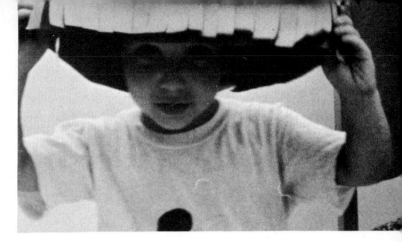

Curtain

ACT III

Scene: *It is late afternoon.* MR. TURTLE, SQUIR-REL, MOLLY MOLE, *and* OWL *are asleep in their homes.*

Curtain

(A strong gust of wind causes the OAK TREE'S *branches to shake wildly)*

OAK TREE
Wake up! Wake up! There is a stranger walking towards us.

*(*SQUIRREL *pops his head out of the tree,* MOLLY MOLE *pops her head out of the ground,* MR. TURTLE *pops his head out of the lake, and* OWL *opens his eyes)*

OWL *(Very mad)*
Can't an owl get a good day's sleep! What is going on in this forest? It must be you,

Squirrel. You have already disturbed my sleep twice today.

SQUIRREL
I was also sleeping, so it could not have been me.

OWL *(Calls from the tree)*
Molly Mole and Mr. Turtle, did you disturb my sleep? It is important that I find the answer to the problem.

MOLLY MOLE
Not me, Owl.

MR. TURTLE
Not me, Owl.

OWL
Then who? Oh my dear, did I just say, "Who?"

SQUIRREL
We must get his attention.

After some whooing and chattering the LITTLE BOY *looks up)*

LITTLE BOY
Hello, little squirrel and owl. I wish I knew

what you were saying. Don't be so angry. It is a lovely day.

SQUIRREL *(To Owl)*
He wants to talk to us.

OWL
We have to turn his attention to the shiny stone.

SQUIRREL
We will have to show him why we are so angry.

*(*SQUIRREL *and* OWL *stand in front of the shiny stone)*

LITTLE BOY
What's this? Oh, it is the aluminum foil I rolled into a ball and used for a catch ball. You are mad because I forgot to take it with me.

*(*MOLLY *and* MR. TURTLE *join* SQUIRREL *and* OWL)*

LITTLE BOY
You too came to complain to me about the aluminum foil ball I left behind. I came back here today because I wasn't sure I cleaned the picnic area. Don't worry, I will take it away from here. I must be extra careful and look high and low for all things that don't belong in the forest. I know I should keep the forest as clean as when I arrived here. Good-bye, friends of the forest.

OAK TREE *(In a mighty voice)*
A stranger walks in the forest. Be very careful. It was the wind and my branches that woke you from your sound sleep.

MOLLY MOLE *(Frightened)*
A stranger! Where?

OAK TREE
Coming closer.

(As the little boy enters the scene, OWL, MOLLY, MR. TURTLE, *and* SQUIRREL *hide in their homes)*

LITTLE BOY
This looks like the place where we had the picnic. *(Looking around)* I think we took all of the paper and food with us.

SQUIRREL *(Pokes his head out of his home. chattering)*
Chatter, chatter, chatter. *(To Owl above him)* So he's the one who placed the smooth, shiny, slippery stone over Molly's home.

OWL
I was correct when I told you I would have the answer today.

SQUIRREL
If it belongs to the little boy he must see it. It might be something special.

OWL
He must take it with him. I am sure the little boy can find a home for this shiniest of stones.

(The LITTLE BOY *leaves the forest with the shiny stone)*

OWL *(Happily)*
I guess that solves both problems. We know who placed the shiny stone on Molly's home . . .

SQUIRREL
. . . and the stone is no longer in the forest.

MR. TURTLE
I am very glad the Little Boy took it with him. It would take me many years to drag it out of the forest.

MOLLY MOLE
If all people would take with them all the things they brought with them into the forest, it would be a cleaner place.

MR. TURTLE
And a beautiful place to visit.

SQUIRREL
And a clean home for us.

MR. TURTLE
Now that the mystery is solved, I'm going back to the pond and snap at a few sunfish.

MOLLY MOLE
A little house cleaning wouldn't hurt. Much sand fell into my home today.

*(*MR. TURTLE *and* MOLLY MOLE *wave good-bye*

to SQUIRREL *and* OWL. *They go to their homes)*

SQUIRREL

It never hurts to gather a few extra acorns for a rainy day. What are your plans for today, Owl?

OWL

I should be on my branch fast asleep. Nighttime will be here very soon. I'll be wide awake. It is all your fault, Squirrel!

SQUIRREL

Since you didn't sleep well today, sleep long and hard tonight. When the birds sing their morning song, you can join me for breakfast.

OWL

Breakfast? That sounds like a good idea. If I can keep my eyes closed and fall asleep, it will be my pleasure to join you in the morning. Did I say good morning? Good day, Squirrel!

SQUIRREL

Good day, Owl. Sleep well, and I will see you at breakfast.

*(*OWL *flies to his branch and* SQUIRREL *hops off into the forest to search for acorns and pine nuts. The forest is quiet and clean once more)*

Curtain

THE END

Good-Bye

Isn't nature fascinating! If you have reached this page, then you have roamed through a kingdom more spectacular than any built by man. You have stood on top of the tiniest grain of sand or in the shadow of a mountain. Things grew before you and a rock-candy crystal became a tasty treat. Nature's discards were changed into beautiful crafts. You should be very proud of yourself. For your achievements and dedicated service to nature, you have the right to wear this "I CREATE WITH NATURE" medal.

Things You Need

scissors
colored construction paper
pencil
tracing paper
paper paste or tape
colored felt-tipped markers or crayons

Let's Begin

1. Cut a circle from colored paper about the size as the medal in the illustration.
2. Trace the ribbon shape from the book onto tracing paper, then cut out the tracing.
3. Use the tracing to draw two ribbon shapes on blue construction paper.
4. Using paper paste or tape, attach the ribbons behind the paper medal.
5. Write the official message on the medal with crayons or colored felt-tipped markers.

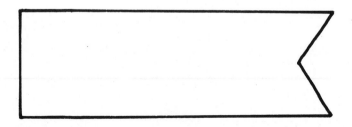